art through litera

Céline George
and
Stephanie Jephson

Acknowledgements

The authors and publishers would like to thank the children of Claremont Primary School, Cross-in Hand Primary School, The Haven Primary School, Mayfield Primary School and Stonegate Primary School for their literacy work and artwork. They would also like to give special thanks to Sophie George and Nicholas Jephson for their artwork.

The authors would like to thank these teachers for their expertise and practical help: Jo Salter, Laura Davies, Jessica Marlow, Peter Pettigrew, Lynda Sheffield, Paul Smith, Angela Hamill, Amanda MacNaughton, Emma Ansell and Sally Fuller. They would like to thank Vicki Brickle for her expert help.

They would like to give special thanks to Sally Nixey, Louise Owen and Jane Wilce for their creative inspiration.

Finally, they would like to thank Maurice Waller and Mary Westhead for their support and advice.

p.54 'Silver' by Walter de la Mare from *The Complete Poems of Walter de la Mare* 1969 (USA:1970). Reproduced by permission of the Literary Trustees of Walter de la Mare and the Society of Authors as their representative.

p.58 'Over De Moon' (28 lines) from TALKING TURKEYS by Benjamin Zephaniah (Viking, 1994) Copyright C Benjamin Zephaniah, 1994. Reproduced by permission of Penguin Books Ltd.

p.66 'Lullaby' Akan, Africa from *Classic Poems to Read Aloud* selected by James Berry (published by Kingfisher).

p.70 'My Pet Grass Snake' by Maurice Waller. Reproduced by kind permission of the author.

Cue for Treason (page 6)

© 2005 Folens on behalf of the authors.

Belair Publications, Apex Business Centre, Boscombe Road, Dunstable, LU5 4RL.
Email: belair@belair-publications.co.uk

Commissioning editor: Zoë Nichols   Editors: Melody Ismail, Caroline Marmo and Joanne Mitchell
Page Layout: Suzanne Ward   Photography: Steve Forest   Cover Design: Steve West

Illustrations: Peter Cottrill p70; Martha Hardy p66; Vanessa Lubach p54; Nicola Pearce p58; Peter Wilks p62.

First published in 2005 by Belair Publications.

Every effort has been made to trace the copyright holders of material used in this publication. If any copyright holder has been overlooked, we should be pleased to make the necessary arrangements.
British Library Cataloguing in Publication Data. A catalogue record for this publication is available from the British Library.

ISBN 0 94788 281 2

Contents

Introduction

Art Through Literacy uses stories, play-scripts, poetry and non-fiction texts as the initial inspiration for work in literacy and art. The aim of the book is to encourage children to express themselves creatively by exploring a range of exciting and challenging activities in both literacy and art. Each chapter begins with a summary of the chosen text followed by useful Starting Points for class discussion. Teachers are able to choose from a range of art and literacy activities that are linked to the text.

The chapters in this book were closely linked to schools' planning in art, design and the daily literacy lesson, using a range of texts from Benjamin Zephaniah to William Shakespeare. Most of the texts were already in place as part of existing literacy plans in schools and this meant that the displays fitted seamlessly into the curriculum. This extra art focus really enhanced the literacy work and made it even more special.

Some of the displays in this book were placed in school libraries along with poetry anthologies, collections of short stories

and playscripts. One school exhibited their displays together in a special classroom for others to visit, rather like an art gallery. In another school, Christmas and greetings cards were made from photographing the displays, giving the work a further practical element.

Using the Texts

The themes in the book are manageable projects that can be completed in two or three sessions. Although we recommend that the displays and literacy activities are completed using a whole-class approach, we suggest that the art and design activities work better in several smaller groups, thus providing the class with a range of artwork at the end of a session. We found that sessions using this approach had a real sense of purpose as everyone in the class contributed to the final outcome.

In the theme on *Earthquakes and Volcanoes*, a whole-class approach was used very successfully. Working with three adults, children completed the work for the main display in one afternoon. The display itself was put up after the session. The theme on *Romeo and Juliet* was completed in the

same way and the children found that working together on such a stunning display, in one afternoon, was both motivating and exciting. With *James and the Giant Peach*, an alternative approach was used where the display was the outcome of half a term's work. It evolved alongside the reading of the story and characters were placed on the display as they appeared in the book. This approach was particularly successful when working with younger children.

Holes, a challenging story, was completed with a smaller group of high-ability children. The display and additional activities were completed in two afternoon sessions using a more focused approach. Using such a modern piece of poetry as *Over De Moon* enabled the children to experience Performance Poetry, which was great fun and highly motivating. This involved one week's work and culminated in a stunning performance of rap poetry, dance and drama.

In this book we have found that by making cross-curricular links with art and literacy, both areas of the curriculum are enhanced. Children of all abilities are able to participate and be very successful and, most importantly, children's levels of motivation have been very high.

We hope you enjoy using this book.

Céline George and Stephanie Jephson

Cue for Treason

This gripping historical novel is full of adventure and intrigue. The key character, Peter Brownrigg, inadvertently discovers a plot to murder the Tudor Queen, Elizabeth I. Together with his friend, Kit, they encounter many obstacles in their efforts to uncover the conspiracy. As the story unfolds, they meet William Shakespeare and perform in his plays with a travelling band of actors. Peter and Kit find out that a peel tower in Cumberland is the headquarters for the treasonous plot and so embark upon the long journey there from London. When they arrive at their destination, Peter overhears some of the conspirators

discussing the details of their plan to kill the Queen in the middle of a performance of Henry V. They have to send the news to the Queen's men, but as the plot unravels they are not sure who to trust.

Starting Points

- Read *Cue for Treason* by Geoffrey Trease (published by Puffin Books). The story could be read as part of guided reading group sessions or by the teacher to the whole class.

- Re-read the first three chapters of the story with the children and discuss the description of the peel tower and its suitability as a place of refuge. Its design offers an excellent view across the surrounding countryside. Pose the following questions: *Why does the shape of the peel tower make it suitable as a lookout tower? Why are there no windows on the ground level? What inspired Peter and his friends to make their own stronghold?*

- In chapter 10, just before the performance of *Romeo and Juliet*, Kit, who has the part of Juliet, disappears, leaving Peter to take on the role. After the performance, Kit returns to give her excuses but gets a cold reception. Ask the children to role-play conversations between Kit and Burbage, and then between Kit and Shakespeare.

- In chapter 12, when Peter retrieves the stolen playscript, he finds that a part of it has been underlined and that a sonnet has been scribbled on the back of it. In the next chapter, we are told part of the meaning of the words. Ask the children to try to work out the hidden code and solve the clue before reading on.

Display

- Paint a Cumbrian background using the description in the book as a guide and place it on a display board. Use sponges and thick paintbrushes to create texture. Print stone shapes on a plain border and add a bold title.

- Using pale grey card, make a peel tower. Draw stone shapes on white paper and paint them by adding black paint to white paint, mixed with sand to create texture. Create a variety of shades of stone. Cut out the stone shapes and stick them onto the peel tower, leaving spaces between them. Add the tower to the display.

- Draw some large rocks on card and create detail using collage materials. Cut them out and place them in the foreground of the display. Peter and Kit can be made using felt and collage materials. Choose appropriate fabrics for their clothes and hair. Cut them out and add them to the display.

Further Activities

- Write a letter from Peter to his parents. The letter should include details of his meeting with Kit, Shakespeare and the travelling band of players. Use the same style as the author so that it would fit seamlessly into the story.

- When Peter first meets Kit, he is rather jealous of her as she gets all the best parts in the plays. Write a short passage, from Peter's point of view, that reflects his feelings at this stage in the story.

- Focus on the beginning of chapter 16 and read up to the point where Peter finds himself on the stairs looking for Tom. All of a sudden, he hears the voices of the conspirators. Stop reading the text at this point and using the voice of the narrator, ask the children to write what happens next.

Art and Design

- Make a textile painting of Peter's home using fabric pastels. Show his mother's washing drying in front of the cottage. Use wool or tweed for the cottage and calico for the clothes. Add buttons and beads to hold the clothes in place. Use embroidery threads and stitches to add detail to the finished painting.

- On page 202 of the book, Kit finds a rose-noble, which is a design of three lilies and a rose on a gold coin. The children could design a floral emblem for a Tudor coin and reproduce it on a large canvas using acrylic paint. Some of the floral emblems could be produced using fabric with stitching to add detail.

- Discuss the style of hats worn during Tudor times and look at examples in books. Make bold drawings of hats showing different shapes and sizes. Cut them out and group together in a mini display.

Fantastic Mr Fox

This is a story about three very mean and nasty farmers called Farmer Boggis, Farmer Bunce and Farmer Bean. Together they hatch a plan to get rid of Mr Fox, who just wants to feed his family and get on with everyone. The farmers plan to catch Mr Fox by setting up camp next to a large tree where Mr Fox lives with his wife and four young children. Boggis, Bunce and Bean are portrayed by Roald Dahl as being utterly ruthless and he tells the reader that they are prepared to shoot, dig out or starve Mr Fox from his woodland home. However, Mr Fox has some plans of his own that might save both his family and the other woodland creatures from the clutches of the three farmers!

Starting Points

- Read *Fantastic Mr Fox* by Roald Dahl, illustrated by Quentin Blake (published by Puffin Books) and read *Fantastic Mr Fox: A Play* adapted by Sally Reid (published by Puffin Books).

- Re-read the first two chapters of the story to the children and then read scene 1 of the play. Discuss the differences between the two texts in terms of layout, stage directions and dialogue. Pose the following question: *In the story the narrator describes the characters of the farmers, but in the playscript a group of children introduce them. Which is the more effective way of presenting them to the reader?*

- Roald Dahl presents Boggis, Bunce and Bean as being greedy and selfish and makes the reader dislike them straight away. Discuss how Roald Dahl's vivid descriptions, use of powerful words and lively dialogue contribute to the overall impression of the characters.

- Read the rest of the play with the children and pose the following questions: *How many ways did the farmers plan to get rid of Mr Fox? Why did Mr Fox's wife think he was fantastic? What do Boggis, Bunce and Bean's ideas for getting rid of the animals tell us about their characters?*

Display

- Cover a display board with blue paper and add a simple border to frame the board. Cut some hills out of green paper and add them to the display. Add some simple line-drawn birds to the sky.

- Make a large tree trunk to cover part of one side – top to bottom – and paint it with several different browns. Use thick paint and different thicknesses of brushes to add texture and depth to the tree. Cut it out and add it to the display. Paint the area of the foxhole using a darker shade of brown.

- Use furry fabric to represent Mr Fox's tail disappearing down the hole.

- Ask three children to draw the characters Boggins, Bunce and Bean on card. Fill in detail using oil pastels and use felt and fabrics for clothes. Cut out the characters and place them around the foxhole on the display.

- Add a spade near to the tree. Make it 3-D by lifting it away from the display using small mounts underneath.

- Add a simple title using a bold font.

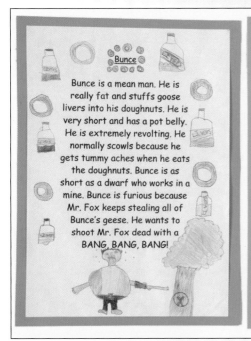

Bunce is a mean man. He is really fat and stuffs goose livers into his doughnuts. He is very short and has a pot belly. He is extremely revolting. He normally scowls because he gets tummy aches when he eats the doughnuts. Bunce is as short as a dwarf who works in a mine. Bunce is furious because Mr. Fox keeps stealing all of Bunce's geese. He wants to shoot Mr. Fox dead with a BANG, BANG, BANG!

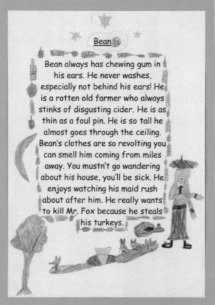

Bean always has chewing gum in his ears. He never washes, especially not behind his ears! He is a rotten old farmer who always stinks of disgusting cider. He is as thin as a foul pin. He is so tall he almost goes through the ceiling. Bean's clothes are so revolting you can smell him coming from miles away. You mustn't go wandering about his house, you'll be sick. He enjoys watching his maid rush about after him. He really wants to kill Mr. Fox because he steals his turkeys.

Boggis scoffs chickens and dumplings all day long. He is fat, stinky and greasy. In fact he is so fat he looks like a weeble! He also has a greasy moustache. He is going to cook Mr. Fox in his chicken stew.

Further Activities

- Focus on scenes 2 and 3 in the playscript, in which Boggis, Bunce and Bean first try to shoot Mr Fox and then they try to dig him out. Using Sally Reid's script as a model for writing, the children could write a short playscript based on one of these scenes. These short scripts could be read aloud or performed to the rest of the class.

- Roald Dahl cleverly links the farmers' appearances to what they like to eat or drink. Using this approach, write a character sketch about one of them. This work could be illustrated.

- Focus on the beginning of chapter 2 in the story where the reader is given a brief description of the setting. We are presented with a simple scene, where on a hill overlooking a valley, in the middle of a wood, stands a huge tree. Ask the children to write a short description of a place of their choice, such as a garden or a park, using the same style as Roald Dahl.

Art and Design

- Discuss the vivid description – at the beginning of chapter 2 – of the place where Mr Fox and his family live. On A5 paper, make a sketch of the described area and fill in the detail using watercolour paints. Place the pictures in a decorative frame to use as greetings cards. Decorate the frames using brightly coloured felt-tipped pens according to the occasion, for example gold and silver for Christmas cards, pinks and blues for other greetings cards.

- Discuss the differences between the three farmers – Boggins, Bunce and Bean. Draw large, pencil-line sketches of the characters, in the style of Quentin Blake, making their differences very pronounced. Use paper collage materials to fill in the detail.

- Discuss the way in which Mr Fox overcame the difficulties of not being able to use his own tunnel exit and ask the children to draw a map of his underground escape route. This could be turned into a board game to be played in small groups. Add detail using oil or chalk pastels and collage materials for areas of exit and entry and for specific landmarks.

- Discuss the various members of Mr Fox's family. Masks could be made to represent them. Keep the masks simple and decorate with collage materials.

Oisín in Tír na nÓg

Tales from Old Ireland is a collection of Irish folk tales and the last story in the book is set in *Tír na nÓg* – the Land of Eternal Youth. The hero of the story is Oisín, who was a great storyteller and musician as well as a brave warrior. When he meets Niamh, the beautiful daughter of the King of Tír na nÓg, he leaves his home and travels with her to the wonderful magical land. He lives happily with Niamh for three hundred years in the palace of the City of Youth but longs to visit his home once again. Niamh warns him that if he gets down from his horse and sets foot on Irish soil he will never return to Tír na nÓg. Oisín sets out on his journey but is disappointed when he arrives in Ireland as everything has changed and his father's castle has become a ruin. He is unable to keep his promise to Niamh and as he sets foot on Irish soil he immediately turns into a very old man. However, before he dies, Oisín tells Saint Patrick all about his adventures and these stories were written down for many generations to enjoy.

Starting Points

- Read 'Oisín in Tír na nÓg' from *Tales from Old Ireland* by Malachy Doyle, illustrated by Niamh Sharkey (published by Barefoot Books).

- Storytelling is a tradition in Ireland and many stories were passed on from one generation to the next through word of mouth. Ask children to sit in a circle and retell the story from memory.

- Pose the following questions: *Why do you think Oisín was so unsettled in the palace of the City of Youth? What did he miss from home? Is it surprising that he felt that everything was too perfect?*

Display

- Back a small display board in sky blue, add a border using tinsel. Cut out two hill shapes – one in dark green and one in light green. Sponge some texture onto the light hill with dark green paint and using a brush add texture to the dark hill with light paint. Add the hills to the board. Paint a dark brown path, cut it out and add it to the light hill.

- Draw the castle using oil pastels, cut it out and stick it to the top of the path on the top of the hill. Cut tree shapes out of green fabric and stick them along the hilltop. Add the trunks using thick, dark paint.

- Cut out the shape of the horse in silky fabric; slightly stuff the fabric before stapling to the board. Add a 3-D saddle and reins using collage materials.

- Make Niamh and Oisín in fabric in a similar way, making them slightly 3-D and adding hair and crowns afterwards. Use contrasting fabric and colours – brocade or velvet in a dark colour for Oisín and something 'floaty' for the princess. Add them to the board.

- Add a title – bold black lettering in a simple script on white paper and add a tinsel trim in either silver or gold.

Saint Patrick meets Oisín and there is a monk writing down the stories Oisín is relating.

Further Activities

- Consider what might have happened if Oisín had not slipped off his horse at the end of the story. The children could write an alternative ending using the author's style.

- Towards the end of the story, Oisín fights the giant in the Land of Virtue in order to rescue the princess. Write another episode, which involves some sort of conflict between Oisín and another giant. Ask the children to use the same descriptive language as the author, so that the new episode fits in seamlessly with the rest of the text.

- The children could write an exciting blurb for the story that captures its magical content.

The princess is being released and Oisín and Niamh are riding home on the pearl white horse. The giant is defeated.

Art and Design

- Discuss the simple but effective way that Niamh Sharkey has illustrated the story. Working in the same style and using coloured inks, ask the children to draw a favourite character. Use watercolour paint to fill in the detail.

- Divide the story into sections and with the children working in groups, draw the sections of the story on A3 paper. Use fabric for the more important areas of the drawings and fill in the small detail using chalk and oil pastels. Place the sections together in sequence on the wall and ask the children to retell the story from the pictures.

Oisín and Niamh are riding to Tír na nÓg. They arrive there and see clear blue skies and sandy beaches.

- Discuss the countryside of the Land of Eternal Youth and the Land of Virtue. The children could use fabric paints on silk to create the landscape of one or the other. Add detail – trees, flowers, sand and lakes – using embroidery thread and simple stitches. Mount the work over a simple wooden frame.

The Pirates of Pompeii

Jonathan was hunting in a green walled garden.

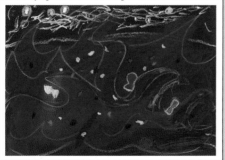
He was flying over wrinkled, indigo-blue silk with dots on it.

Tigris led him to a broad river, with trees on either side.

This story is set during Roman times in AD79 – just after the eruption of Mount Vesuvius and its devastating effects. It is about four friends, Flavia, Jonathan, Nubia and Lupus, who discover that many children are disappearing from the refugee camp where they live. Their determination to solve the mystery involves a dangerous encounter with pirates and slave dealers. Ultimately, the story is about friendship, loyalty and forgiveness.

Starting Points

- Read *The Pirates of Pompeii* by Caroline Lawrence (published by Dolphin Paperbacks).

- Focus on the opening page of the story and pose the following questions: *What dramatic event has just taken place at the beginning of the story? Why were there charred tree trunks instead of olive or palm trees? Why was the landscape described as the Land of Grey?*

- Throughout the story, at different times, Jonathan thinks he has already seen in a dream what is about to happen. Focus on pages 21, 22, 26 and 27 of the book. Jonathan's dreams are inspired by music and especially by Nubia playing her lotus-wood flute. In the dream, he is transported to another world, where he is able not only to run faster than before, but also to fly. Discuss what Jonathan did and saw during this wonderful dream.

- Focus on pages 106–108 of the book, where Felix shows Flavia a beautifully painted, ceramic, drinking cup. He tells Flavia how the image depicted on the cup represents a magical story about the god Dionysus. Pose the following questions: *Can the story of Dionysus be linked in any way to the main story? Why did Dionysus change the pirates into dolphins? Felix gives Flavia the beautiful cup as a gift. What does this tell the reader about Felix's character?*

He saw a ship with a red-striped sail, and children on the deck.

On the other side of the river was a city made of jewels.

Display

- Divide an A3 piece of sketch paper into six parts. Ask the children to make a small series of preliminary drawings to create a storyboard in black and white depicting the chosen sequence of events in the dream. Use these sketches to produce the pictures for a display.

- On black sugar or pastel paper draw the outline of the first image in the dream sequence. Add in detail using oil and chalk pastels. Outline and embellish using gold and silver felt-tipped pens.

- Ensure the children follow closely the colours described in the book and keep the pictures simple, bold and of a similar style reflecting the mood of the dream.

- Add a relevant quote from the book, which could be word-processed. The pictures could be displayed in sequence on the wall; include a title.

Below him was a blue cove, a crescent beach, and tents.

Further Activities

- In this story, the four key characters are influenced by others in different ways. Flavia's treatment of Nubia, for example, is influenced by Pulchra's unkind treatment of Leda. Ask the children to write a short piece in a speech bubble about how they think they might respond in a similar situation.

- Focus on Jonathan's dream sequence and, using brainstorming, notes and diagrams, compile a list that shows the dream sequence. The children could present it with an illustrated border depicting some of the images from the dream.

- When we first meet Pulchra, Felix's eldest daughter, she appears rather a selfish child, who is used to getting her own way. As the story unfolds, her character develops and becomes kinder. The children could write a character sketch of Pulchra that shows these changes.

I wouldn't have done the same thing Pulchra does to her slave. If I were a slave and I was treated that badly I would feel very sad. I think Nubia's life has changed because a moment ago she was being treated nicely and now she is being treated badly.

Art and Design

- Roman soldiers were very well protected when they went into battle. Discuss the armour they wore and select one of the items to illustrate using mosaics cut from a variety of different-coloured papers.

- Make a 'catalogue' of Roman armour, showing up-to-date modifications that might improve the safety of the soldiers in battle. Use a computer to print out the catalogue, along with appropriate pricing, and display it in the classroom.

- Working in groups, complete a large sketch of a Roman shield. Discuss the decoration that might have been added to it and fill in the detail using a variety of different-textured fabrics cut into mosaic-sized squares.

- The Romans wore distinctive helmets. Discuss how and why they were made, and working in groups produce some replicas for display. Use a digital camera to record the process in sequence, from design to completion.

- Discuss the weapons used in battle and look at images of swords. Ask the children to select one image and make a design for a print. Make a series of prints exploring overprinting and colour combinations.

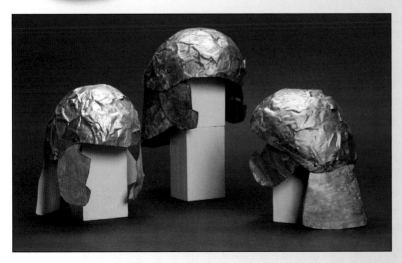

The Mother Who Turned to Dust

This African creation myth tells the story of how a star sees a green and blue planet in a faraway corner of the universe and longs to go and live there. The star is granted three wishes by her father, the Sun, and, in turn, she has to shed all her brilliant powers and glittering coat of pure light if she wants to live on the green and blue planet. When the star lands on the planet, she is amazed at its natural beauty and vivid colours. Her first wish is to have many children; this is granted and she becomes the Mother of All Children. As the story unfolds, the children change and become selfish and start to misuse the beautiful green and blue planet. This causes the Mother of All Children great sorrow and upon her death her second wish is granted: that her remains are covered in black and that she is permitted to continue serving her children. Finally, her third wish is granted and she turns into the silvery moon who keeps watch over her children.

Starting Points

- Read *The Mother Who Turned to Dust* from *Nelson Mandela's Favorite African Folktales* by Kasiya Makaka Phiri, illustrated by Jonathan Comerford (published by W.W. Norton & Company).

- Discuss how the author uses figurative language, in particular personification, to create such a vivid image of the Mother of All Children and to convey her caring and compassionate nature.

- Read aloud the Mother of All Children's song on page 122 of the book and discuss how precious and precarious our planet Earth really is. Pose the following questions: *What is the green and blue planet? How did the Mother of All Children care for her children? What advice does the Sun give his daughter when her children start to behave selfishly? Why did the children cut down the trees and dig pits in the ground? What is the moral of this myth?*

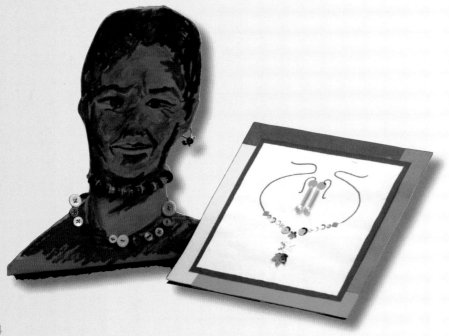

Display

- Cover a display board with black paper.

- Make a large planet out of blue card. Use tissue paper to represent the countries on Earth. Alternatively, draw the rough outlines of various countries and fill in the detail using collage materials to represent land, trees and mountains. Use tissue paper and fabric for the sea.

- Add the Milky Way to the top of the display using splatter paint. Add a small Sun far away to one side at the top.

- Cut out the shapes of the items taken to the planet by the star in the story, decorate them and add them to the display. Alternatively, make some large paintings of the items taken to the planet and add these with labels to the display.

- Make the Mother of All Children using paint and coloured paper, cut her out and add her to the display. Add some jewellery. Add a title to the display. The children could then add some appropriate words or morals gained from the book to spaces in the sky.

Further Activities

- Ask the children to make notes on the outline of the story and, using these as a guide, to take turns at telling the story in pairs.

- Using the themes of Mother Earth and the importance of looking after our planet, ask the children to write their own versions of this myth using figurative language, such as personification and simile, to create a vivid scene. Suggest that they choose different stars as the main characters but use the 'green and blue planet' as the main setting.

- Ask the children to use their versions of the myth as a starting point for oral storytelling. The children's stories could be made into a collection of illustrated myths and placed in the school library for others to enjoy.

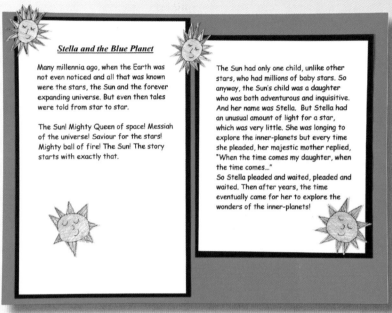

Stella and the Blue Planet

Many millennia ago, when the Earth was not even noticed and all that was known were the stars, the Sun and the forever expanding universe. But even then tales were told from star to star.

The Sun! Mighty Queen of space! Messiah of the universe! Saviour for the stars! Mighty ball of fire! The Sun! The story starts with exactly that.

The Sun had only one child, unlike other stars, who had millions of baby stars. So anyway, the Sun's child was a daughter who was both adventurous and inquisitive. And her name was Stella. But Stella had an unusual amount of light for a star, which was very little. She was longing to explore the inner-planets but every time she pleaded, her majestic mother replied, "When the time comes my daughter, when the time comes..."
So Stella pleaded and waited, pleaded and waited. Then after years, the time eventually came for her to explore the wonders of the inner-planets!

Art and Design

- Discuss the descriptive colours that the daughter of the Sun saw in 'the many colours of the light that had come with her from home'. Using as many of the colours as possible, with a combination of watercolour paints and oil pastels, the children could create an abstract picture of the planet as it was, when the star first arrived.

- Ask the children to use pen and ink or watercolours to sketch either the daughter of the Sun or The Mother of All Children, referring to the descriptions that are given in the story. Discuss how she changes throughout the story and what has caused the changes.

- Discuss what gradually happened to the planet as the children grew and moved away. Working as a class, make a large collaborative collage of the planet – 'then and now'. Discuss with the children how the destruction could have been avoided and what might be done to return the planet to its former glory.

- Discuss the images we are given of the daughter of the Sun in all her finery. The children could design some jewellery based on the various descriptions. Make some of the designs using collage materials on paper, or actual 'jewels' – beads, buttons, sequins, old jewellery – and string them onto thin wire. Display these on a simple cut-out card model of the daughter of the Sun.

- Discuss the various items that the daughter of the Sun took with her to her new home. Make a 3-D item – water pot, cooking pot, basket or mat. Use clay or papier mâché to make the pots and try weaving strips of fabric, wool or old plastic carrier bags to make the mat, and plaiting the strips before coiling them into baskets.

The Legend of the Bluebonnet

This thought-provoking legend is based on the culture and beliefs of the Comanche People and outlines the origin of the Texas state flower, the bluebonnet, which is a wild lupine. The story has a strong moral message and reminds the reader of how important it is to look after and respect the Earth. Ultimately, the story focuses on the courage and selfless action of a young girl, who is prepared to make a personal sacrifice in order to save her people.

Starting Points

- Read *The Legend of the Bluebonnet* by Tomie DePaola (published by PaperStar).

- The story opening is a prayer to the Great Spirits requesting them to end the drought and send rain in order to restore life. The dancers implore the spirits to tell them what they have done to cause so much anger that has led to the dreadful famine. Discuss with the children the effectiveness of this opening and how it draws the reader into the story from the start.

- The use of figurative language to describe the little girl's parents and grandparents as being like shadows is a powerful image. It conveys a wistful sense of loss, sadness and love. We are also given a vivid description of the child's doll, which was made for her by her mother, and the blue feathers decorating it, collected by her father. Discuss the importance that special toys have for children and why they are so precious.

- In the story, the wise man, called the Shaman, speaks to the people and tells them the reason for the famine. He insists that the Great Spirits want a sacrifice in the form of a burnt offering of a most valued possession. Pose the following questions: *How did She-Who-Is-Alone get her name? What does She-Who-Is-Alone do when she hears the Shaman's words? What happened when the child scattered her doll's ashes to the Home of the Winds? Why were the flowers blue? When the Comanche People saw the beautiful, blue flowers they gave the little girl another name – One-Who-Loved-Her-People. Why was it an appropriate name for her?*

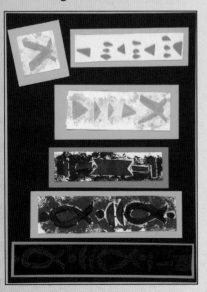

Display

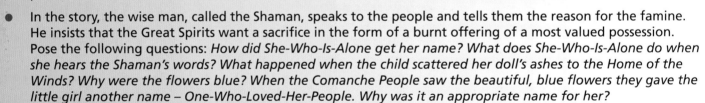

- Cover the top half of a design board with pale blue paper for the sky. Cut out some hill shapes in green and add them to the display. Discuss the bold, bright patterns that appear on totem poles and print some borders in the style of these totem poles. Add them to the sides of the display. Alternatively, cut out some paper dolls – the kind that hang together when unfolded – and add them as a border to the display.

- Make a few, blue, tissue paper flowers and place them on the hills. Using a sponge, paint more bluebonnet flowers on the hills further away.

- Make some 3-D tepees and add them to the display. Add grass to the foreground – use paint and thick brushes, tissue paper, sponges or a combination of all three to add texture.

- Create a small fire – use card for the logs and tissue paper or foil for the flames and add it to the display.

- Draw some characters from the story, including She-Who-Is-Alone, and fill in the detail using oil pastels. Cut them out and add them to the display. Raise the drawings of the characters away from the display to add depth.

- Using fabric, make a small 3-D doll for She-Who-Is-Alone to hold. Add a bold title to the display.

Further Activities

- Ask the children to write a story plan for a legend using the same theme as *The Legend of the Bluebonnet* but with a different main character.

- Using the style of the author, the children could write another version of the legend with a different setting. Include a prayer as the story opening, with the use of figurative language to create vivid images and a strong moral as a message to the reader.

- Write a short piece describing the girl's feelings about her doll and its appearance. The children could write in the first person and illustrate the work.

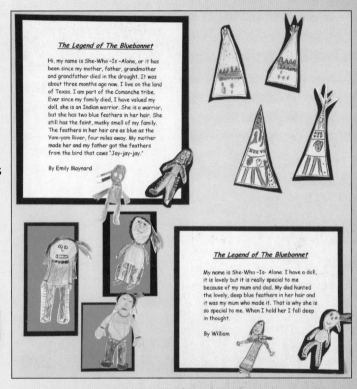

Art and Design

- Ask the children to do some observational sketches of bluebonnets/lupines. Use soft pencils to shade the sketches and then repeat the sketches using pastels. Discuss the differences between using pencil and colour.

- Study the shape and colour of some bluebonnets/lupines. Do simple line drawings of the flowers and use the drawings as a pattern for cutting the shapes out of fabric. Create a 'textile sketch' by placing several fabric flowers together in a cut-out fabric container – this could be either 2- or 3-D.

- Working in groups, the children could make up a circular design of a favourite flower or plant. Use bold primary colours to fill in the detail. Cut the circle into six segments and swap amongst the children in the different groups. Reform the circular design and discover what kind of kaleidoscope design appears. Mount these as a mini display of flowers in a garden.

- Using their knowledge of the flowers, ask the children to design a two-colour pattern that could be printed on paper or fabric.

The Selfish Giant

At the beginning of this story, the main character, the Selfish Giant, refuses to share his beautiful garden with the local children and forbids them from playing there. It is a tale of contrasting themes: winter and spring, coldness and warmth, joy and sadness, selfishness and generosity. As time passes and the seasons change, the Giant comes to realise the importance of sharing. The ending is a powerful one, with a special message of love and hope.

Starting Points

- Read *The Selfish Giant* by Oscar Wilde (published by Puffin Books).

- Focus on the story opening where Oscar Wilde uses powerful language to create a vivid setting. Ask the children to imagine the colours that are used at the start and to write an alternative story opening, which will fit in with the rest of the story.

- Discuss why the Giant's actions appear to have such a dramatic effect on the seasons in his garden, where spring becomes an endless winter.

- Discuss the effectiveness of Wilde's use of personification when he introduces the reader to the Snow, who is covering up the grass with her white cloak. The Frost is painting the trees silver and the North Wind is wrapped in furs, roaring about the garden with Hail, dressed in grey, causing havoc.

- Ask the children to imagine the colours used in the story to depict the chilly weather conditions and to emphasise the tense, bleak atmosphere, such as greys, whites and silvers.

Display

- Look at paintings and photographs of natural forms, such as trees and blossoms. Discuss their line, shape, colour and texture. Ask the children to carefully draw trees, focusing on shape and texture. Choose one of their drawings to develop into a design for display purposes.

- Use wax crayons to make bark rubbings for the tree. Scrunch up pieces of newspaper to form the shape of the tree. Cover the tree shape with the bark rubbings.

- Divide the display board into two sections, one representing spring and the other representing winter.

- Make tissue paper flowers for the spring side of the tree and curl strips of green paper for the grass.

- Place white tissue paper on the branches for the winter side of the tree and sprinkle silver glitter on the ground for snow.

- Add a printed brick wall along the base of the board and create a title from twigs.

Further Activities

- Ask the children to create short, descriptive pieces of writing that evoke the different ways winter can transform the landscape. Use Oscar Wilde's descriptions for inspiration.

- The children could add personification to their descriptions to make the writing even more powerful.

- In the story, the Giant displays a notice, which reads 'Trespassers Will Be Prosecuted'. Ask the children to write a persuasive letter to the Giant, from their point of view, explaining why the garden has become such a dismal place since they have been banished from it. Include in the letter reasons why they should be allowed to play in the garden once again.

- Create a book containing children's story openings and place it in the school library for others to share.

Art and Design

- Discuss with the children how the landscape looks in the winter and paint 'wintry pictures' using foam brushes and watery paint. Add glitter and sponge snow onto the finished work. Try the same thing with spring landscapes, using thicker paint and brighter colours.

- The children could sketch a simple landscape on calico. Cut fabric in simple shapes and glue it to the sketch. Add stitches to represent grass, blossom, fences, cloud shapes, birds – anything the children might associate with the landscapes. They could create either winter or spring scenes.

- Draw a line down the centre of a piece of calico and create a winter/spring collage using fabric. Add detail by using pictures torn out of magazines – flowers, trees, grass and so on.

Holes

In Louis Sachar's book, *Holes*, the main character, Stanley Yelnats, has been wrongly accused of stealing a pair of trainers. As a punishment for his crime, he is sent to a juvenile detention centre for young offenders. The story is set in Camp Green Lake, which is in the middle of a vast American desert landscape, inhabited by deadly yellow-spotted lizards. As Stanley learns to cope with the harsh conditions of Camp Green Lake, he makes friends with Zero and frees his family from a long running curse. The resolution of events is a resounding victory for good over evil and a reassertion of the values of friendship, honour, family and perseverance.

Starting Points

- Read the story *Holes* by Louis Sachar (published by Bloomsbury). The story could be used as a text for guided reading. Focus on the descriptive writing in chapter 8 of the book, where the author gives a detailed account of what the deadly yellow-spotted lizard looks like.

- Discuss with the children how Louis Sachar's use of descriptive language in chapter 8 of the book presents us with a very clear image of the yellow-spotted lizard and its behaviour.

- Discuss the effectiveness of Sachar's use of dialogue and narrative to depict and develop characterisation. He uses dialogue to inform the reader about the relationship between the two main characters, Zero and Stanley, and how their relationship changes as time passes.

- Produce a class book of short stories, using Louis Sachar's distinctive style, which contains new episodes for the story, including flashbacks to convey the passage of time. The children should write in the third person, past tense and with a balance of narrative and dialogue.

Display

- Cover the display area with paper that the children have painted with thin paint and thick brushes to create the impression of a desert sky.

- Add a hilly landscape that has been painted green.

- Make a desert landscape in the foreground using sponges and thick paint, using as many different shades of brown and yellow as possible.

- Create holes by cutting paper and fabric into circles.

- Make the lizards by sticking green fabric to a lizard shape drawn onto card. Add texture using buttons, beads, scraps of torn paper, ripped fabric and thick paint. Lastly, add the yellow spots made from paper, fabric or buttons. Bend the lizards in half (to make them 3-D) and add to the display.

- Add a large painted Sun and a title using cut-out letters.

Further Activities

- If possible, watch the film version of *Holes* (Walt Disney Productions) and ask the children to write a review, based on how characters are depicted, the setting and how 'time slips' are handled. Reviews should include suggestions for how the film could be made even more dramatic.

- The children could write a letter from Stanley to his mother explaining what life is like in Camp Green Lake. In the letter, the children should try to put themselves in Stanley's shoes, remembering that he is an American boy, whose parents think he has gone to a sort of holiday camp.

- Ask the children to write a short piece of descriptive writing about Camp Green Lake's surrounding barren wasteland, with its numerous scatterings of holes and its grim conditions.

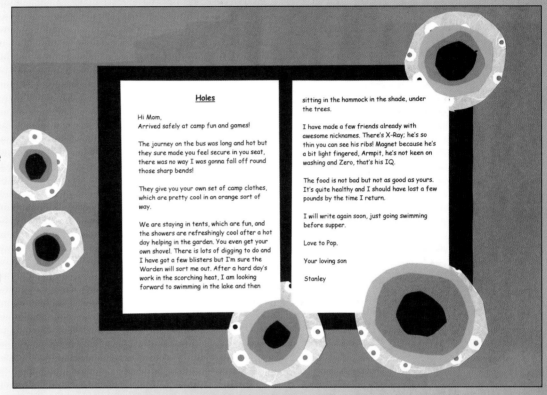

Holes

Hi Mom,
Arrived safely at camp fun and games!

The journey on the bus was long and hot but they sure made you feel secure in you seat, there was no way I was gonna fall off round those sharp bends!

They give you your own set of camp clothes, which are pretty cool in an orange sort of way.

We are staying in tents, which are fun, and the showers are refreshingly cool after a hot day helping in the garden. You even get your own shovel. There is lots of digging to do and I have got a few blisters but I'm sure the Warden will sort me out. After a hard day's work in the scorching heat, I am looking forward to swimming in the lake and then

sitting in the hammock in the shade, under the trees.

I have made a few friends already with awesome nicknames. There's X-Ray; he's so thin you can see his ribs! Magnet because he's a bit light fingered, Armpit, he's not keen on washing and Zero, that's his IQ.

The food is not bad but not as good as yours. It's quite healthy and I should have lost a few pounds by the time I return.

I will write again soon, just going swimming before supper.

Love to Pop.

Your loving son

Stanley

Art and Design

- Make a lizard landscape. Create outline sketches of lizards on card. Using a variety of materials, fill in the outline of each lizard to achieve a layered effect. The children could use wax crayons, tissue paper, bubble wrap and wool to create texture. Embellish with buttons for eyes and yellow fabric for the spots. Using frayed hessian as a background, stitch across it with a combination of wool, torn fabric strips or ribbon to create the landscape. Glue the lizards to the hessian background.

- Discuss the reasons why Stanley was sent to Camp Green Lake, particularly focusing on the issue of the stolen trainers. On an A4 piece of paper, ask the children to draw a detailed sketch of a trainer. Transfer the outline of the same trainer onto a larger piece of card and use paper torn from magazines to build up the collage, adding a lace for the final touch.

- Produce pastel paintings of the setting of Camp Green Lake, with colours reflecting the barren wasteland, dotted with numerous holes and roasted by the relentless heat of the Sun.

Swan Lake

This enchanting story is based on the composer Tchaikovsky's original 1877 ballet, where true love conquers all and the ending is a happy one. The story opening describes a young prince enjoying life without a care in the world. On the night before his eighteenth birthday, he holds a party to celebrate with his friends. During the party, a flock of swans fly past and the prince and his friends decide to take their bows and arrows to hunt the birds. However, during the chase, the prince remains behind by the lake to rest and within moments, a most beautiful woman appears before him. She tells him that she is the Swan Queen he tried to kill moments before and she goes on to explain how she and her friends had been transformed into swans by an evil sorcerer. As the story unfolds, we discover that true love is more powerful than any evil spell.

Starting Points

- Read *Swan Lake* retold and illustrated by Lisbeth Zwerger (published by North-South Books).

- At the beginning of the story, we are told that the prince's mother was not very happy with him. Pose the following questions to the children: *Why was the prince's mother not pleased with him? What did she want the prince to do at the ball?*

- During the ball there is a sudden change of atmosphere when two people, dressed in black, enter the ballroom. The language used is very dramatic and Lisbeth Zwerger uses short, sharp sentences to convey tension. Discuss the author's use of language with the children and its effect on the reader.

- Throughout this story, the weather is used to create atmosphere. Towards the end of the story, there is a flood and the Swan Queen is pulled into the water. Discuss other times in the story when the weather mirrors what is happening and the impact this has on the reader.

Display

- Cover a display board with pale blue paper on the top half and cream paper on the bottom half. Add some stage curtains from fabric to the sides and top of the display in place of a border. Alternatively, paint a scene from the book and use it as the background for the display.

- Ask the children to draw some couples dancing and to fill in the detail with oil pastels. Keep the colours pale and muted so that the couples blend into the background of the display. Cut them out and place them on the board. The children could also make a group of puppets or dolls from fabric and use them as the extra dancers at the ball.

- Make a chandelier from collage materials. Use beads that shimmer and glitter to make the ballroom special.

- Make two large 3-D ballet dancers as the main characters of the story. Colour them with fabric paints or crayons and add fabric clothes and embellish with beads, buttons and so on. Attach them to the display and add a title.

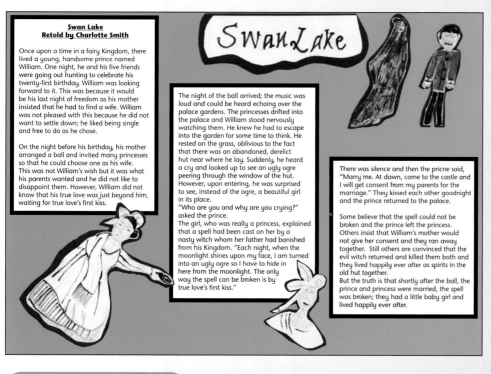

Swan Lake
Retold by Charlotte Smith

Once upon a time in a fairy Kingdom, there lived a young, handsome prince named William. One night, he and his five friends were going out hunting to celebrate his twenty-first birthday. William was looking forward to it. This was because it would be his last night of freedom as his mother insisted that he had to find a wife. William was not pleased with this because he did not want to settle down; he liked being single and free to do as he chose.

On the night before his birthday, his mother arranged a ball and invited many princesses so that he could choose one as his wife. This was not William's wish but it was what his parents wanted and he did not like to disappoint them. However, William did not know that his true love was just beyond him, waiting for true love's first kiss.

The night of the ball arrived; the music was loud and could be heard echoing over the palace gardens. The princesses drifted into the palace and William stood nervously watching them. He knew he had to escape into the garden for some time to think. He rested on the grass, oblivious to the fact that there was an abandoned, derelict hut near where he lay. Suddenly, he heard a cry and looked up to see an ugly ogre peering through the window of the hut. However, upon entering, he was surprised to see, instead of the ogre, a beautiful girl in its place.
"Who are you and why are you crying?" asked the prince.
The girl, who was really a princess, explained that a spell had been cast on her by a nasty witch whom her father had banished from his Kingdom. "Each night, when the moonlight shines upon my face, I am turned into an ugly ogre so I have to hide in here from the moonlight. The only way the spell can be broken is by true love's first kiss."

There was silence and then the pricne said, "Marry me. At dawn, come to the castle and I will get consent from my parents for the marriage." They kissed each other goodnight and the prince returned to the palace.

Some believe that the spell could not be broken and the prince left the princess. Others insist that William's mother would not give her consent and they ran away together. Still others are convinced that the evil witch returned and killed them both and they lived happily ever after as spirits in the old hut together.
But the truth is that shortly after the ball, the prince and princess were married, the spell was broken; they had a little baby girl and lived happily ever after.

Further Activities

- Listen to Tchaikovsky's ballet *Swan Lake* before and during the following writing activities.

- Using the same style as the book, ask the children to write an alternative ending to this story.

- The children could do an extended piece of writing using the idea of a spell being cast on a group of friends, which changes them into swans. Suggest to the children that a different plot could be introduced and perhaps a different setting. This work could be presented in a class anthology and illustrated in the style of Zwerger's *Swan Lake*.

Art and Design

- Listen again to some music from the ballet *Swan Lake* by Tchaikovsky. Using oil pastels, ask the children to convey the movement of the music with pattern. Use appropriate colours to match the mood of the music.

- Look at pictures of dancers concentrating on line, tone, shape and the colours that convey movement. The children could paint a picture of one or more dancers in a similar style or use oil pastels.

- Discuss the shape, form and movement of a swan, either in flight or whilst swimming. Working in groups, ask the children to produce a simple dance sequence that replicates these movements. Using a digital camera, take group photographs of the children performing these sequences and display these with the pictures of dancers (see above).

- The children could make 3-D swans out of mod rock and add detail using acrylic paint and collage materials.

The Beginning of the Armadilloes

In this short story by Rudyard Kipling, the characters are jungle animals living near to the turbid Amazon River. The opening of the story introduces Stickly-Prickly Hedgehog and Slow-Solid Tortoise, who are enjoying life grazing on the banks of the river. The reader is also introduced to a Painted Jaguar who eats everything he can catch and to Mother Jaguar, who teaches her young son about how to eat hedgehogs and tortoises. When the Painted Jaguar meets Stickly-Prickly Hedgehog and Slow-Solid Tortoise they realise how naïve he is and try to outwit him. In the end, we meet the Armadillo.

Starting Points

- Read *The Beginning of the Armadilloes* by Rudyard Kipling (published by Macmillan Children's Books). Focus on Kipling's use of repetition in phrases such as Best Beloved and High and Far-Off Times, which is rather old fashioned and formal. Talk about the onomatopoeic use of additional adjectives to describe some of his animal characters, such as Stickly-Prickly Hedgehog and Slow-Solid Tortoise.

- Ask the children to write a short descriptive piece using Kipling's style and base it on a well-known story with animals as characters. Focus on the beginning of the story and ask them to illustrate it.

- In Kipling's story, there are very strong relationships between the animal characters. The Hedgehog and the Tortoise work together to outwit the Painted Jaguar, who is rash and naïve. The Painted Jaguar, who is learning to stand on his own two feet, needs his mother's support and she gives him guidance in a kindly and loving manner. Discuss the importance of these relationships with the children.

Display

- Back a display board in light green paper. Use green and brown wax crayons to create a turbid river on white paper, painted over with a blue wash.

- Using as many different greens as possible, cut painted strips of paper and curl them to form grass and leaves and attach these to the display.

- Use brown wool to stitch bark patterns into a strip of Hessian for the tree trunk. Stuff this from behind once it has been added to the display and add leaves and branches of curled paper. Paint large leaves for the tree top on thick paper, cut them out and add them to the display to create depth.

- Look at illustrations and photographs of armadilloes, concentrating on shape, colour and pattern. Ask a group of children to do a large outline drawing of an armadillo on thick card. Fill in the detail using paper and foil. Add triangle shapes to the base and feet of the armadillo. Use fabric for the ears and long pointed nose, and add tiny buttons for eyes.

- Alternatively, use a variety of different-textured paper (tissue paper, poster paper, foil) and build up the surface of the armadillo by grading the size of the cut paper and layering it in a decorative way. Decorate these areas with buttons, beads and sequins.

- Place the armadillo on the jungle display and add a title using triangles of foil to make the letters.

Further Activities

- Ask the children to write a short piece of additional dialogue to fit into the end of the story.

- Choose a well-known illustrated story that has animals as its main characters and retell the beginning of the story, setting the scene and introducing the characters in Kipling's style.

- The children could choose any incident from the story and rewrite it, using the first person, from the point of view of any one of the animal characters.

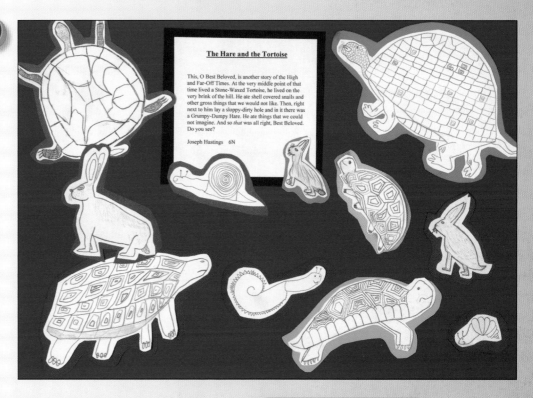

Art and Design

- Discuss the animals in the story and ask the children to make a model from playdough or clay of a favourite character. The models could be embellished with buttons, beads and sequins.

- Talk about the river in the story. Ask the children to think about the patterns that appear on water when something is dropped into it. Try to recreate these patterns with paint or crayon. Experiment with different papers and techniques.

- Discuss different techniques and materials the children might use to illustrate the animals in this story (pastels, pencil, paint, chalk, printing, drawing) and ask them to choose to illustrate part of the story.

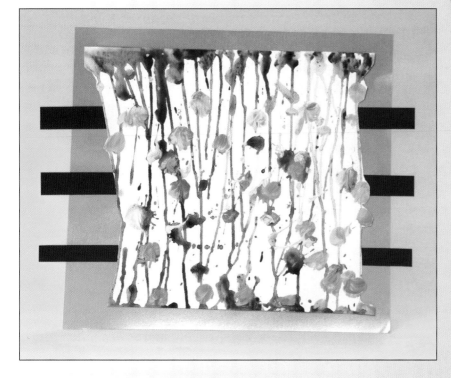

The Giant's Necklace

In *The Giant's Necklace*, the story takes place during a family holiday in which Cherry, the main character, decides to make a giant's necklace out of cowrie shells from the local beach. On the last day of the holiday, she remains alone on the beach after the others have returned home to pack. Cherry is determined to finish collecting, as she wants to complete the necklace. Engrossed in her search, she is totally unaware of the approaching storm. Trapped by the incoming tide, Cherry is cut off from the beach and clambers up the rocks for safety; but the power of the sea is too much for her and what happens next is both incredible and tragic.

Starting Points

- Read *The Giant's Necklace* by Michael Morpurgo (published by Egmont). Focus on the ending when Cherry returns to the cottage to find it full of uniformed men drinking tea around the kitchen table with her family. Discuss how helpless Cherry must have felt seeing her family so distressed. Discuss with the children how Cherry's family might have felt when they saw her towel full of the shells she had been collecting.

Display

- Cover the display area with white paper.

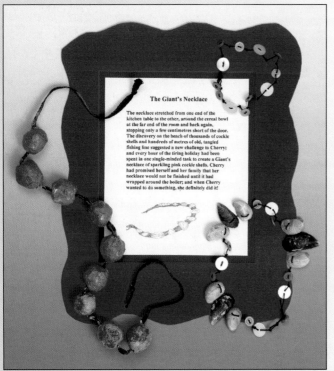

- Discuss the colours that the sky and sea might be during a storm. Use as many of these colours as possible and paint on A4-sized paper using sponges and foam brushes. Cut the sky into 2cm squares and stick these tiles onto the display board to represent the sky.

- On a separate sheet of large paper, use a mixture of thick and thin paint in a variety of browns and paint the cliffs. Use thick brushes and sponges to add texture to the cliffs. Tear along the top of the paper to represent the craggy edges of the cliff tops. Add the cliffs to the display, making sure that the craggy tops cover the sky.

- Add sand to thick paint for the sea. Paint strips of blue paper with swirling strokes to represent the stormy incoming tide. Add texture to the waves by sponging some swirls with glitter glue and/or white paint. Add the strips to the display, laying them in rows beneath the cliffs.

- Using coloured paper, tear out the shape of a cottage and glue this to the display above the cliffs.

- Make a necklace using shells and add this to the bottom of the display.

- Include a bold title by sticking torn paper pieces over pencilled letters. Cut these out and arrange them on the cliffs.

Further Activities

- Ask the children to write the beginning of the story with the same setting and characters, but to choose something other than a necklace for Cherry to make. Discuss the different objects that have been chosen and whether or not they are as effective as the necklace.

- The children could write endings for the story using a different narrator, such as one of Cherry's brothers.

- Choose a section from the story set in the mine and, working in twos, the children could write the story in the form of a script with stage directions to set the scene and to indicate how the actors need to say their parts. When the scripts are finished, perform a selection of them, in a dramatic way, to the rest of the class.

- Look at paintings that depict a stormy seascape, discuss the composition in terms of colour, texture and movement. Write a short descriptive piece, which captures the mood of the storm.

Art and Design

- Make a collection of things that might be found on the beach. Arrange them in a display and produce pencil sketches. Ask the children to use a viewfinder to focus on one area. Using torn coloured paper, enlarge the area into an abstract cameo of the still life.

- Discuss how the children might make a necklace using shells collected from the beach. Allow them to experiment with different materials, such as buttons, shells and papier-mâché beads to make a variety of necklaces.

James and the Giant Peach

James Henry Trotter is a four-year-old boy whose parents are eaten up by a rhinoceros. He is sent to live with his wicked aunts, Spiker and Sponge, in a bleak house within a desolate garden – they treat him very unkindly. One day his luck suddenly changes. He meets a magician who gives him a small, white, paper bag containing a selection of extraordinary things. The magician explains how to make a magic potion that will make wonderful things happen to James. As a result of the magic, a peach appears on the peach tree in the garden and it starts to grow at lightning speed to an incredible size. That is when James's exciting adventures really begin.

Starting Points

- Read *James and the Giant Peach* by Roald Dahl, illustrated by Quentin Blake (published by Puffin Books).

- Focus on the first chapter of the story and discuss how the mood changes from one of tranquillity to one of deep unhappiness. Talk about the effectiveness of Roald Dahl's use of similes and adjectives to create a vivid scene. For example, when describing James's bedroom Roald Dahl says 'His room was as bare as a prison cell …' This evokes feelings of bleakness and emptiness that James experiences in his new home. Challenge the children to find other examples of similes in the text.

Display

- Cover a display board in peach-coloured paper and add a large green paper hill to the centre of the display. Create a border of cut-out paper peaches.

- Paint a cottage and stick it on the hilltop. Add other features to the scene, such as a fence, path and grass made from collage materials.

- Make the peach tree by painting green leaves and sticking these to a brown paper trunk on the background. Create some peaches, life-size, using tights. Stuff them with tissue paper and paint them light orange, then add them to the tree.

- Make a large 3-D peach using painted calico or cotton. Stuff it while stapling it down to the display board. Add a fabric twig and leaf, stuck down the middle to give a 3-D appearance.

- Add the rest of the characters (made from collage materials) and a large title to the display using fabric letters.

Aunt Sponge   Aunt Spiker

Further Activities

- Write a story opening using Roald Dahl's style of figurative language and powerful adjectives. The children should use the same setting as *James and the Giant Peach* but think of other ideas for the disappearance of James's parents and create new characters in place of Spiker and Sponge. They could then read aloud their story openings in a dramatic way, using musical instruments to enhance the text. Record the readings onto a story tape for others to listen to.

- Write a class review of *James and the Giant Peach* and illustrate it using wax crayons and watercolour paints.

Art and Design

- Using wax crayons, cover the surface of an A4 piece of white sketch paper with bold, colourful patterns. Paint over the paper with black paint and let it dry. Ask the children to scratch away a picture of the beautiful house where James lived with his mother and father.

- Using watercolour paints, the children could paint the view that James might have seen from Aunts Sponge and Spiker's hilltop house.

- On A4 paper, ask the children to draw a portrait of Aunt Sponge or Aunt Spiker. Fill in the detail using only black felt-tipped pens and thick and thin lines.

- Working in groups, record a gathering of all the animals in the story. Let each member of the group select an animal and draw it on A4 card. Fold the card in half to make it stand up. Create a collaborative picture by grouping the finished drawings in front of a cut-out painting of a peach.

The Cay

The story of *The Cay* deals movingly with issues of racism, survival and how relationships develop and change over time. It is set during the Second World War and is told in the first person from the point of view of Phillip. Phillip is travelling on a ship, with his mother, from Panama to Miami when it is hit by a torpedo. Phillip is knocked on the head by a plank of wood and becomes temporarily blind. He finds himself on a makeshift raft in the middle of the sea along with an elderly man called Timothy and a cat called Stew. After some days adrift on the sea, they find themselves stranded on a remote Caribbean island, which they call 'The Cay'.

Starting Points

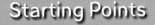

- Read *The Cay* by Theodore Taylor (published by Puffin Books). Discuss how Phillip's attitude to Timothy changes as the story unfolds and how their friendship develops during their time on the island. Ask the children for their views about Phillip's prejudice against Timothy at the beginning of the book.

- Timothy teaches Phillip how to survive in the harsh living conditions on the island. This is a difficult task because of Phillip's blindness. Arrange role-play activities where children are asked to put themselves in Phillip's shoes and pose questions about his feelings.

- Towards the end of the story, as Timothy gets physically weaker, Phillip becomes the stronger of the two and we begin to witness their role reversal. Discuss how this change helps Phillip to cope on the island on his own.

Display

- Divide a display board into three sections. Cover the top third of the board with a painted sky – blue at the top fading to pale blue on the horizon. Add the green island background to the middle.

- Cut some hills into the top of the green. Use sponge painting to add texture to the island. Glue sand to yellow paper to give texture to the bottom third of the board. Add a yellow border.

- Create a 3-D palm tree using corrugated cardboard cut into segments and placed over one another. Add some palm leaves, made from tissue paper to the top of the trunk. Make coconuts using fabric and stuff them before adding to the tree.

- Make Phillip and Timothy using collage materials and attach them to the display on small box mounts to raise them away from the board for a 3-D effect. Add a title to the display.

Further Activities

- Ask the children to write some additional dialogue to fit the end of chapter 3, when Phillip starts to blame his mother for his predicament. Encourage the use of a mixture of narrative and dialogue in the style of the writer, which reflects Timothy's West Indian accent.

- Writing in the author's style and in the first person, the children could write in character – as Timothy – the episode from the story where Phillip climbs the palm tree for coconuts.

- Keep a class diary, which records the children's feelings and thoughts about the story as it unfolds.

Art and Design

- Discuss the raft that Phillip and Timothy made. Ask the children to create a pictorial list illustrating the things the characters collected for the raft and put them in order of importance.

- Discuss the hut that is built on the island. In pairs or groups, ask the children to create a pen and ink sketch of the hut and its surrounding landscape on A3 paper. Still working in groups and using the sketch, ask them to paint an aerial view of the island.

- Use painted stones and other collage materials to form the word HELP. Incorporate this into a model of the island with stand-up palm trees, sand and shells made from a variety of collage materials. A raft could be made from twigs and string.

Goodnight Mister Tom

In this evocative story, William Beech, a young boy, is evacuated from London to the countryside because of the bombing raids during the Second World War. In the village of Little Weirwold, William meets Tom Oakley, a widower, who takes him in out of duty. As the story unfolds, the pair become inseparable. Tom discovers the awful underlying truth behind William's obvious anxiety, and the reason for Tom's reluctance to talk about the past is also revealed. This moving story has its share of tragedy and joy and so reflects accurately the dreadful consequences of war on both children and adults alike.

Starting Points

- Read *Goodnight Mister Tom* by Michelle Magorian (published by Puffin Modern Classics).

- Focus on the beginning of the story where the author gives a vivid description of William as a pale, sickly-looking boy. In contrast, Tom is presented as being healthy and robust with a shock of bright, white hair. Talk about the effect of Magorian's powerful words to convey William's nervousness, such as clutching, shivered, shaking fingers, frightened and lonely. Pose the following questions: *Why does William feel so ill at ease?*

- Show the children the film version of the story up to the part where Tom goes to London to find William. Re-read chapter 16 of the book, The *Search*, and discuss the contrast between the beginning of the chapter, which is set in the pretty village of Little Weirwold, and the setting of Tom's arrival in London. Pose the following questions: *Why did Tom find it difficult to understand what the Londoners were saying? What were the main differences between the countryside and London?*

Display

- Split a display board into two, one half for Little Weirwold and the other for London. Back both halves in appropriately coloured paper and add a border in black, blue and green.

- Paint aeroplanes of varying sizes and add these to the sky in the London area. Create a sky background on this side showing a bombing raid. Add a bombed street of terraced houses made from paper and collage and junk materials.

- On the other side of the board create rolling hills from green backing paper, sponge-painted to give texture. Use pastels to draw Tom's cottage and the rest of the village. Add tissue paper flowers and leaves to stems and place in rows in front of the cottages.

- Add a title and a signpost in the centre to label the two halves of the display.

Further Activities

- Ask the children to retell the opening of the story with two different narrators, firstly from William's point of view and then from Tom's. When William is the narrator, they should include his impressions of Tom and the cottage where he lives. With Tom as the narrator, include his description of William's appearance and demeanour. Ask them to use a balance of narrative and dialogue and to write in the past tense in the style of the book.

- The children could compare how the book and its film version (1998) deal effectively with character development, plot and the final outcome. They could create a chart to show the similarities and differences. For example, in the film, the setting is visible but there is no narrator.

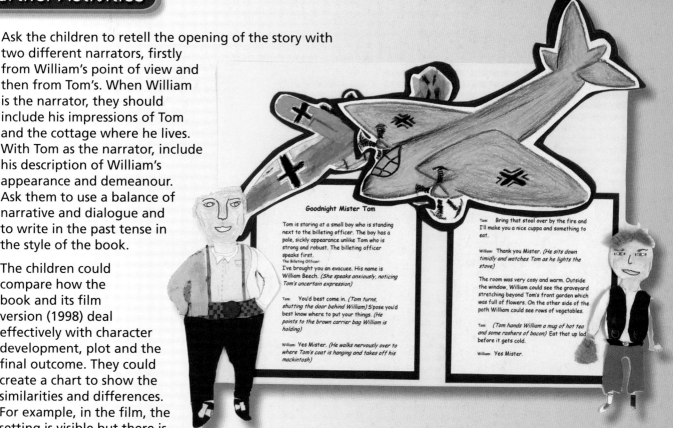

Art and Design

- Discuss the descriptions of evacuees in the opening chapter of the book – the clothes they wore, the luggage that they took with them, their overall appearance and how they were transported to the country. On A4 sketch paper ask the children to draw an evacuee as they arrive at their new home.

- Divide an A3 sheet of paper in half width-ways. On the top section draw the home an evacuee might have left behind in London. Fill in the detail using inks and fine brushes. On the bottom section draw the home an evacuee has arrived at in the country. Fill in the detail using oil or chalk pastels to emphasise the contrast in living conditions.

- Talk about the differences in food that the evacuees may have found between the town and the country. Make two still life compositions of foodstuffs – tinned and powdered foodstuffs contrasting with fresh fruit and vegetables – and paint still life pictures. Display in two groups titled 'Town' and 'Country'.

- Discuss how evacuees carried their gas masks with them at all times. The children could make a 3-D box that could contain a gas mask. Ask them to create a leaflet containing instructions for using the gas mask.

Beyond the Deepwoods

This book is set in the Deepwoods, a dark and mysterious place full of unexpected and perilous happenings. The Woodtrolls are some of the many creatures living there. Although Twig, the main character, is not a Woodtroll, he is adopted by Spelda and Tuntum Snatchwood. Twig faces many exciting adventures and meets some wonderful characters like the Banderbear and also some terrifying ones like the Wig-Wigs. Two of the prominent themes that run through this book are: appearances are not always what they seem and kindness can be found in unexpected places.

Starting Points

- Read the story *Beyond the Deepwoods* by Paul Stewart and illustrated by Chris Riddell (published by Corgi Books). Focus on chapter 8 when Twig meets the Banderbear. Ask the children the following questions: *Why was the Banderbear howling in pain when Twig first saw him? Why is Chris Riddell's illustration of him so effective?*

- Paul Stewart describes the dangerous and nasty Wig-Wigs as being rather sweet looking. On the other hand, the Banderbear, who appears at first to be very menacing, is a kind and gentle creature. Discuss the fact that looks can be deceiving and the effect the portrayal of these characters has on the reader's initial thoughts about them.

- Paul Stewart uses powerful verbs to create tension and to maintain a quick pace, full of action and suspense, which holds the reader's interest. Discuss his use of language, especially in the build-up to helping the Banderbear.

Display

- Back a display board with brown paper and a yellow border. Draw a pencil line to represent the path disappearing into the distance. Ask the children to sponge the path with dark brown paint to look like mud. Sponge or paint the area to the front of the picture green to represent grass in the woods.

- Add some tree trunks made from paper painted with thick paint. Draw some trees using pastels and place them on the display as trees in the distance. Include some pastel-painted branches too.

- Draw large images of Twig and the Banderbear and fill in the detail using collage materials.

- Draw some Wig-Wigs on paper. Fill in the detail using different shades of wool and add bugle beads for the Wig-Wigs' teeth. Add to the display.

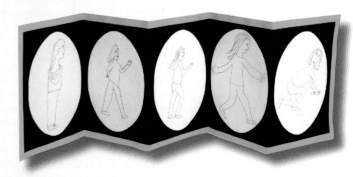

Further Activities

- Using Paul Stewart's style, ask the children to write a short paragraph about what happens after Twig takes out the Banderbear's rotten tooth. Encourage them to use dialogue, narrative and powerful verbs to set the tone.

- The children could write an account of the game of Trockbladder that Twig played, from the point of view of his friend, Hoddergruff. They should include the rules of the game and describe how Twig was treated once he strayed from the path and scored a goal.

- Ask the children to describe Twig's character and appearance using the text and Chris Riddell's amazing illustrations as inspiration.

Art and Design

- Discuss the way in which *Beyond The Deepwoods* is illustrated, noting the use of fine lines to add detail and shading. Focus on the characteristics that make Twig unique – his hair, his height and the clothes he wears. On A4 sketch paper, ask the children to sketch Twig and fill in the detail using coloured ink.

- Discuss the way that the Banderbear moved. The children should work in pairs, taking turns to pose in a similar way to that of the Banderbear, and record the poses in simple line sketches. Cut out the poses and stick them onto brightly coloured card in a moving sequence.

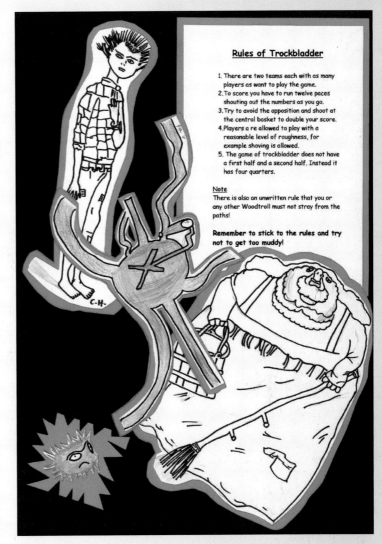

Rules of Trockbladder

1. There are two teams each with as many players as want to play the game.
2. To score you have to run twelve paces shouting out the numbers as you go.
3. Try to avoid the opposition and shoot at the central basket to double your score.
4. Players are allowed to play with a reasonable level of roughness, for example shoving is allowed.
5. The game of trockbladder does not have a first half and a second half. Instead it has four quarters.

Note
There is also an unwritten rule that you or any other Woodtroll must not stray from the paths!

Remember to stick to the rules and try not to get too muddy!

- Talk about the changing appearance of the orange Wig-Wigs from nice to nasty. Create 3-D Wig-Wigs from a circle of calico or hessian, and ask the children to stitch the pieces of paper and fabric onto the circle, overlapping them like scales to imitate fur. Sew and stuff the circle to make a 3-D body. Add big buttons for eyes and bugle beads for teeth.

Kensuke's Kingdom

The story is told from the point of view of Michael, a young boy who describes how he sets off around the world with his parents and his dog Stella in a yacht named *Peggy Sue*. Michael and Stella fall overboard and are rescued by Kensuke, an elderly Japanese gentleman, who lives on a remote, uninhabited island, and provides them with food and water. After a while, they become great friends and Kensuke teaches Michael all about Japanese culture – how to paint, to wear a kimono and also about life in Japan. Eventually, Michael is rescued by his parents but Kensuke decides to remain on the island and asks Michael not to tell anyone about him for ten years.

Starting Points

- Read *Kensuke's Kingdom* by Michael Morpurgo (published by Egmont). The opening of the story is both mysterious and intriguing. It cleverly refers to some sort of promise linking a flashback sequence to ten years ago. Ask the children the following questions: *Who is Kensuke? What is so special about him? Why did Michael disappear and how was he rescued? Why did Kensuke ask Michael to promise not to tell anyone about him for ten years?*

- In chapter 10, Michael Morpurgo describes how Kensuke gathers his friends, the orang-utans, around him by singing to them. He compares the scene to the Pied Piper leading children to the mountain. Talk about the comparisons between the two (perhaps read the poem on page 62 if unfamiliar with the story) and ask the children to pinpoint what they have in common.

Display

- Cover a display board in cream/white paper or use a hessian-backed board.

- Make a large 3-D Kensuke – draw the outline on fabric/paper. Paint the hands, arms, feet, legs and face. Add hair, beard (wool) and other facial detail using paint/stitches. Stuff the figure as it is being stapled to the board for a 3-D effect. Cut out a kimono from fabric and add it to the figure. Make Michael in a similar way.

- Paint a cherry tree in Japanese style onto the backing paper and add tissue-paper blossoms.

- Make a table using a cardboard box. Create three saucers from card (one for octopus ink, one for water, and the third for mixing the two together) and place them on the table stapled to the front of the board.

- Place a framed Haiku poem on the display.

- Add the title in Japanese-style script down each side of the display.

Further Activities

- Kensuke painted a cherry tree over and over again because it reminded him of his sister. The children could write a sequence of Japanese Haiku poems either to reflect the beauty of the cherry tree and its blossom or to tell Kensuke's life story. Write the poems in the present tense using three lines totalling seventeen syllables. The first line has five syllables, the second has seven and the third has five.

- At the beginning of the story Michael tells us that he kept a ship's log to record events on his journey. Ask the children to write a final log entry, which expresses Michael's feelings about being rescued and leaving Kensuke behind.

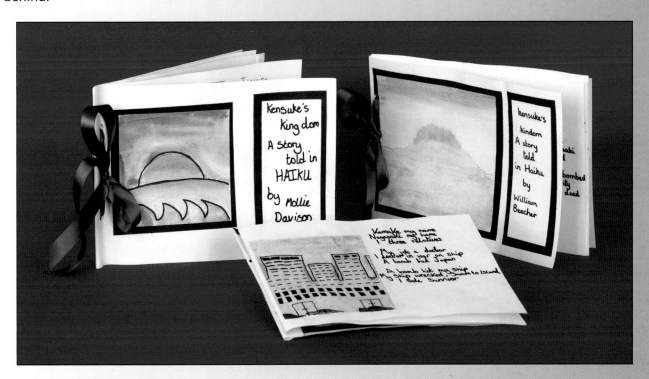

Art and Design

- Discuss the importance of cherry trees to Kensuke, and his approach to painting them. On A3 paper and working in pairs/small groups, ask the children to sketch a large cherry tree. Fill in the detail/texture of the trunk with watercolour paints and add the blossom using collage materials.

- Discuss the way Japanese artists approach their work. The children could paint or print in a similar style. Talk about how their work could be mounted as an exhibition in an art gallery. They could design the cover of a catalogue for the exhibition or a poster to advertise and promote an exhibition of their work.

- Look at the patterns on Japanese kimonos. Design a kimono, front and back, on kimono-shaped paper. Transfer the design onto fabric using fabric paint. Cut out the back and front of the kimono and stitch together.

The Other Side of Truth

In Beverley Naidoo's novel, *The Other Side of Truth*, we are presented with serious issues about injustice and lack of freedom. The beginning of the story is set in Lagos, Nigeria, where dramatic events quickly lead to the main character, 12-year-old Sade, and her younger brother Femi, being forced to leave their country because of their journalist father's outspoken views. The story centres on their survival in unfamiliar surroundings, along with their determination to be reunited with their father and also to ensure that the truth will be told.

Starting Points

- Read *The Other Side of Truth* by Beverley Naidoo, (published by Puffin Books). Discuss the children's feelings about Sade and Femi's predicament. Encourage them to empathise with the characters and to comment on their feelings of isolation and loneliness.

- Discuss Beverley Naidoo's style of writing, with a focus on her use of figurative language to create an effective image. Examine and find examples of passages that deal with issues such as lack of freedom of speech, the plight of the refugee, bullying in school and how finding out the truth about people can lead to greater understanding and tolerance.

Display

- Divide the display board into two sections – the top with green paper and the bottom with grey paper. Make a silhouette of the London skyline using a variety of shapes and sizes and stick it to the grey section.

- Add some bright tissue paper flowers and fabric leaves to the background of the green section.

- Draw some faces of general characters – school children, street people – and cut them out. Attach them to the green background.

- Decide which characters are linked with Sade and Femi's home in Nigeria and which are linked with London. Using a variety of fabrics, cut out circles, run a stitch around the edge and gather slightly. Stuff the circles lightly and gather them up a little more. Add details to the faces using collage materials. Stick the 'Nigeria' faces to the top of the display and the 'London' faces to the bottom. Add labels showing their names and a title using cut-out newspaper letters.

Further Activities

- The children could write a back cover blurb for the book or write a review of the story and place it in the school library.

- Ask the children to rewrite an episode from the story using Femi as the narrator.

- Beverley Naidoo gives minor characters made-up names, which reflect their appearance or occupation, such as Mr Fix-It, Brass Buttons and Pepper-Red Lips. Using this technique, write stories with a similar style and voice, which convey either a sense of loss or the feeling of being an outsider in an unfamiliar setting.

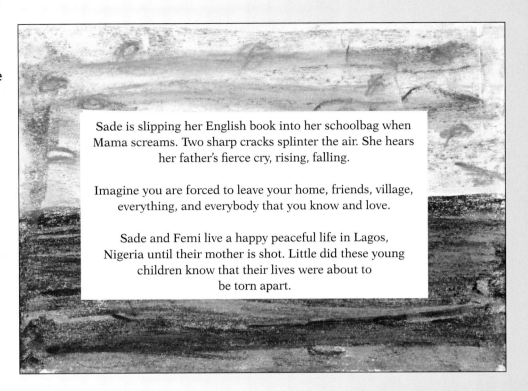

Sade is slipping her English book into her schoolbag when Mama screams. Two sharp cracks splinter the air. She hears her father's fierce cry, rising, falling.

Imagine you are forced to leave your home, friends, village, everything, and everybody that you know and love.

Sade and Femi live a happy peaceful life in Lagos, Nigeria until their mother is shot. Little did these young children know that their lives were about to be torn apart.

Art and Design

- Use a variety of materials to make a model of Sade and Femi's home in Nigeria.

- Ask the children to draw an aerial view of Sade and Femi's village – what they might have seen from the aeroplane if they had left during the day.

- On A4 paper, draw one of the characters. Stitch features into a calico face and stick this onto the drawing. Add wool/string hair and fabric clothes. Cut out carefully and mount. Arrange the characters, standing up in a group scene. Add a background, for example a school, a London street scene or a village.

The BFG

In this story, Roald Dahl introduces the reader to a world of giants and dreams, along with many exciting adventures. One of the key characters in the story is Sophie, a little girl who is snatched by the BFG in the middle of the night from the village orphanage where she lives. The BFG is a very kind and thoughtful giant and unlike the other nasty giants in the story, he protects Sophie and shows her how to catch and mix dreams. The characters are larger than life and are either very good or very

bad, with wonderful names that reflect the sort of people they are. The BFG and Sophie become true friends and set out to rid the world of cruel and nasty giants forever.

Starting Points

- Read *The BFG* by Roald Dahl, illustrated by Quentin Blake, and read *The BFG: Plays for Children* adapted by David Wood (both published by Puffin).

- Focus on the opening three chapters of *The BFG* in which Sophie is snatched in the middle of the night, then read the first play scene *The Snatching of Sophie* and compare the story opening with its play version.

- Focus on the chapter 'The Bloodbottler' in which the BFG and Sophie have a terrifying encounter with the huge, disgusting Bloodbottler giant. Pose the following questions: *Why did the Bloodbottler force his way into the BFG's cave? The Bloodbottler did not like the taste of the snozzcumber and spat it out along with Sophie. What did he really like to eat?*

- Although the Bloodbottler and the BFG are both giants, they have nothing else in common. Ask the children to describe the ways in which they are different.

Display

- Cover a display board with grey paper. Cut some strips of brown paper and add as shelves to the display. The children could draw some pictures of jars filled with dreams, cut them out and stick them onto the shelves.

- Make a 3-D table top from card and add it to the display.

- Create a trumpet using card, a closed suitcase in the same way and add these to the display with a small fishing net.

- Make a tiny Sophie and a very large BFG from collage materials.

- Ask the children to fill some real jars (ensure safety) with 'dreams' made from tissue paper and feathers. Stick on labels about each dream and put them on the 3-D table top on the display.

Further Activities

- Focus on the chapter 'Dreams' and using Roald Dahl's style – unusual words, vivid descriptions and a sense of fun – the children could write their own dreams in the form of an illustrated list.

- Using the play as a model for writing, choose part of a chapter from the book with plenty of dialogue and write it in the form of a playscript. The children could work in groups and each group could choose a different section. These short play scripts could be read aloud or performed to the rest of the class.

- Ask the children to write a vivid description of an imaginary giant and think of a suitable name. Illustrate these.

- Make a glossary of giant vocabulary as a class.

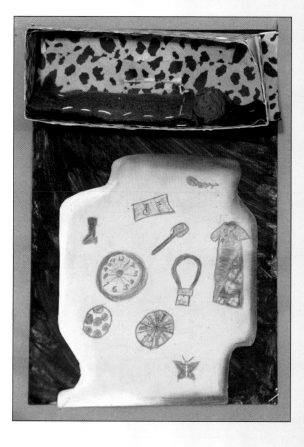

Art and Design

- Focus on the 'Dreams' chapter in the book and discuss any dreams the children can remember. Illustrate them using chalk pastels. Merge the colours using fingers to give a dreamlike smudgy look to the pictures.

- Look at Magritte's painting 'The Reckless Sleeper' and discuss it with the children, along with their own dreams. Ask them to illustrate their dreams in the style of Magritte's painting using sketch pencils and paint or coloured inks to fill in the details. The pictures could be displayed inside a box, with a clay model of a sleeping child's head covered with a fabric blanket in the foreground.

- Discuss the images that appear in one of the dreams in the book. Develop a simple design from one of them and make a print block. On a large piece of coloured paper create a multicoloured print dream sequence.

- Discuss the amazing descriptive words that the BFG uses when talking about the dreams he catches. The children could illustrate some of these words using coloured ink sketches and collage materials.

The Butterfly Lion

This story is about a young boy called Bertie who rescues an orphaned white lion cub. The scene is set in South Africa and Bertie and the cub become inseparable until the day Bertie is sent to boarding school in England. The lion cub is sold to a circus owner and is taken to France as a star attraction. Many years later, the white lion is found again by Bertie and their friendship is rekindled. As the mysterious story unfolds, it is the Butterfly Lion who ensures that their friendship will never be forgotten.

Starting Points

- Read *The Butterfly Lion* by Michael Morpurgo and illustrated by Christian Birmingham (published by Collins).

- Focus on the chapter 'Timbavati' and discuss how Michael Morpurgo evokes sympathy for Bertie by portraying him as an only child who is restless and wants to explore the world outside the confines of his parents' compound. Pose the following questions: *Why does nobody believe Bertie about the white lion cub? How does Bertie feel when his parents don't believe him?*

- At the beginning of the chapter 'Bertie and the Lion', Bertie has to leave the compound in order to rescue a lion cub being stalked by a group of hyenas. Pose the following questions: *What would you have done in Bertie's position? Do you think he was brave to stand up to the hyenas? Why did Bertie's mother come out after him armed with a rifle?*

Display

- Back a board with white paper and paint on a grey sky. Cut a hill shape out of green paper and place it across the lower half of the display board.

- Ask a child to draw the lion on card and fill in the detail with white tissue paper. Cut it out and place the lion onto the hillside.

- Use brightly coloured paper to make some kites. Stick the kites to boxes and add to one side of the display. This will give a 3-D impression. Add string tails and tissue paper bows.

- Draw some African animals using chalk pastels, cut them out and add them to the display.

- Make some 3-D butterflies – use pipe cleaners to form the shape and cover with several shades of blue tissue paper. Make the butterflies in several sizes and add them to the display, the larger ones towards the bottom and the others flying towards or settling on the lion. Also draw some butterflies using wax crayons, cut them out and add to the display.

Further Activities

- Ask the children to write a brief character sketch of Millie and focus on the small details Michael Morpurgo uses to convey her appearance and the language he uses to create such a vivid image of her character.

- The children could write about how they would have responded if they had been in Bertie's shoes watching the lion cub surrounded by hyenas.

- Ask the children to write about any experience they have had involving looking after an animal. Create leaflets explaining how to look after a pet properly.

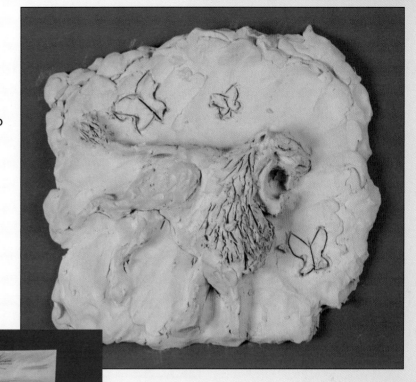

Art and Design

- Look at landscape artist Tony Hudson's images of Africa. Using either oil or chalk pastels, and working in a similar style, do a picture of the area where Bertie lived in Timbavali.

- Draw a large lion, or other African animal shape, on colourful A3 paper. Make a butterfly print using string, or cut a butterfly shape out of a tile and fill in the animal shape using blue paint.

- Discuss how the Butterfly Lion was carved into the hillside. On A3 card, build up a hillside scene using tissue paper and sketch a lion onto it. Fill in the detail with collage materials. Add an outline using thick white wool.

- Working on soft wood or clay, carve a model of the Butterfly Lion.

The Roman Record

The Roman Record is a non-fiction text, which covers a variety of stories about Roman times. It combines historical information about the Romans with an accessible, journalistic style, making it both interesting and factual.

Starting Points

- Read *The Roman Record* (published by Usborne) and focus the children on its visual presentation, such as the use of headlines, the different fonts used for sub-headings and headlines, the general layout, writing in columns and the use of pictures with captions.

- Look at the headlines in the book and talk about how they grab the reader's attention by being dramatic and eye-catching. Headlines are crucial in a newspaper and they should grab the reader's attention with a hint of what the story is about. Sometimes newspaper pictures stand on their own with a longer caption but with no story included. Such pictures tell their own story and need to be very striking. Look at examples of these from the book or from real newspapers.

Display

- Cover a display board with white paper. This display should look like a newspaper page that is opened out – add lines top and bottom to indicate this.

- Select some of the children's work about Romans and mount it like a newspaper article. Add the work to the display.

- Add some 3-D 'photographs', for example make a volcano using collage materials – stuffed slightly from the back to give a 3-D effect. Draw a senator and add his clothes using fabric draped like a toga.

- Add a title using large print and a simple script.

- Write all captions in large letters and vary the sizes as in a real newspaper. Use the same script throughout.

Further Activities

- Ask the children to do some research on the Internet or in the school library about the eruption of Mount Vesuvius. Using the same journalistic style as *The Roman Record*, they could write a report about the actual eruption of Vesuvius and how it affected the people who lived there. They should include in the article an eyewitness account of what happened and convey a sense of urgency by presenting the story as if the news is just coming in. Include a dramatic headline for the report.

- The children could choose a picture that conveys a powerful image, either from *The Roman Record* or from another source on the Romans, and write a clever caption to go with it.

- Use IT to draft the reports and to organise the layout. Edit the stories to fit into a particular space.

Art and Design

- Discuss the designs that the Romans used in their mosaics to decorate the rooms in their homes. The children could design their own Roman pattern to decorate an eating vessel/plate. Replicate the design as a mosaic on a paper plate using cut paper tiles.

- On A4 card, draw the outline of the Roman Senator, Livius Impluvius. Cut it out carefully, making two templates – a positive and a negative. Select one of the templates and place it on an A3 sheet of poster paper. Add colour, either inside the negative template or on the outside of the positive template, using a sponge and thick paint to produce an image. Repeat the sponge impression several times using different colours to create an abstract picture.

- Ask the children to draw a simple outline of some Roman crockery or an impressive Roman building. Use brightly coloured oil pastels to fill in the detail. Cut the picture up and then stick it back together on white paper, leaving a thin white line around all the pieces.

Earthquakes and Volcanoes

This non-fiction text, *Earthquakes and Volcanoes*, gives a clear and concise account of scientific research explaining how earthquakes occur, what happens during one and how they are measured and monitored. It offers a helpful guide to understanding the nature and incredible power of this natural phenomenon.

Starting Points

- Read *Earthquakes and Volcanoes* by Fiona Watt (published by Usborne). Pose the following questions: *What causes earthquakes? What are the physical effects of earthquakes? What are the human effects of an earthquake?*

- Look at other examples of non-fiction explanatory texts and discuss the following features of impersonal writing: Use of present tense and passive voice: *As an earthquake strikes and the ground begins to tremble, buildings are shaken in all directions;* text divided into linking paragraphs with appropriate choice of formal connectives: *furthermore, however, therefore* and *consequently;* use of technical vocabulary: *epicentre, vibrations, landslides, seismometers, hazards* and the *Richter scale;* use of the third person and formal vocabulary: *Scientists estimate that over 800 000 earthquakes occur every year.*

Display

- Cover the display area with grey paper. Draw two lines to show the perspective of the street, with a vanishing point slightly above the halfway mark of the board.

- Paint a road area with large cracks and holes. Paint the pavement area in the same way, adding cracks with pencil lines. Paint the sky area with sponges using grey and white, with a little red and orange to represent fires and heat.

- Draw some buildings – some damaged and some undamaged. These could then be stuck onto the background area of the display board. Stick some of the buildings onto boxes of different sizes to add a 3-D element. Glue these buildings to the front of the picture on either side of the road.

- Add pieces of wood to help give the buildings a distressed look. Use pipe cleaners to make lamp-posts and black wool for electrical wires and run these along the street. Use torn tissue paper as water flowing from pipes, and fine fabric and organza/netting stuffed with cotton wool to represent smoke and steam rising from the road and broken pipes.

- Add pictures, either cut from magazines or drawn by the children, of damaged cars and shop goods that might end up in the street.

Further Activities

- Working in pairs, ask the children to write an explanatory text on earthquakes using the following sub-titles as a guide for each of the linking paragraphs: Introduction, Causes, Natural causes, Physical effects, Human effects, Results, Conclusion.

- Ask the children to create a role-play about what should be done in the event of an earthquake.

- Build up a collection of magazine and newspaper articles that show the devastation that an earthquake can cause and how the various authorities cope with restoring life to normal.

- Visit the library and use the Internet to research more information about earthquakes. Retrieve information and make some quick notes.

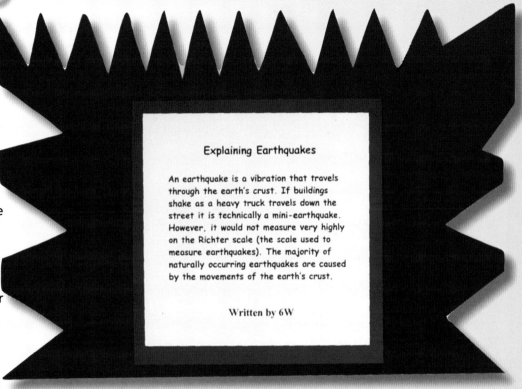

Explaining Earthquakes

An earthquake is a vibration that travels through the earth's crust. If buildings shake as a heavy truck travels down the street it is technically a mini-earthquake. However, it would not measure very highly on the Richter scale (the scale used to measure earthquakes). The majority of naturally occurring earthquakes are caused by the movements of the earth's crust.

Written by 6W

Art and Design

- Think about life during and after an earthquake and discuss the colours associated with this. Colour-wash two pieces of A4 paper and once this has dried, ask the children to do quick pen and ink sketches of the landscape during the earthquake.

- Make a 3-D picture using scrunched-up tissue paper to portray the broken landscape after an earthquake. Add pictures of buildings, cars and people roughly torn out of magazines.

- Use charcoal and grey paper to draw pictures of buildings affected by an earthquake.

On the Trail of the Victorians in Britain

This non-fiction text presents a variety of Victorian photographs, postcards and illustrations together with some contemporary photographs of Victorian buildings to bring this fascinating part of our history to life. The layout of the book is clear with useful suggestions for further research work on the subject.

Starting Points

- Look at the layout of *On the Trail of the Victorians in Britain* by Peter Crisp (published by Franklin Watts) and focus on the contents page, the main sections with their headings, the glossary, the timeline and the index page. Explain how to use these sections in the book by skimming and scanning the text in order to become more familiar with the contents and to locate information with confidence.

- Focus on the chapter 'Schools' on pages 22 and 23. Read through this section carefully with the children and ask the following questions: *What did many poor children have to do instead of attending school? In the 1870s, hundreds of board schools were built for poor children where boys and girls were educated separately. What clues are we given that prove this? Before the board schools were built, there were ragged schools for the poorest children – how did these differ from the board schools?*

Display

- Ask the children to design some floral wallpaper in the style of William Morris and to cover the top half of a display board with it. Their designs could be drawn onto a sheet of A4 paper and then colour-photocopied to produce enough sheets to cover the board.

- Add a narrow strip of brown paper to represent the picture rail and a piece of felt to represent a carpet to the bottom of the display board. Make a Victorian fireplace and add a fire of logs and flames made out of card, tissue paper and foil. A 3-D mantelpiece could be added made from stiff card.

- Draw a rocking horse onto card. Colour it in and cut it out and stick it onto the display. Alternatively, cut some furniture out of card and stick it onto the display. Make slightly puffy seats for chairs and give tables 3-D tops.

- Add a sampler or small piece of sewing to hang from the picture rail and add a mirror made from foil above the mantelpiece.

Further Activities

- After class discussion and using the book as a source of information, make some notes on the differences between the lives of children working in factories and those from middle-class families. Convert these notes into a short report for others to read, with an emphasis on presentation, clarity, conciseness and impersonal style.

- Using the Internet as a source of information, ask the children to find out about the designer William Morris and to write a concise explanatory account about his designs and what inspired his work. They could illustrate the writing using one of William Morris's designs.

Art and Design

- The children could design some Christmas wrapping paper using William Morris's style as a starting point. Print the wrapping paper and use it to wrap up a present at Christmas.

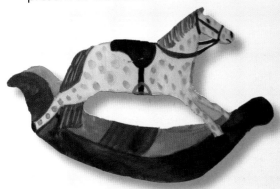

- Discuss the ways in which the Victorians decorated their bedrooms, and what furniture and toys would be in the room. Draw a postcard-style picture of a child's bedroom and fill in the detail using collage materials.

- Look at pictures of homes for the workers, middle-class homes and homes for the wealthy. Ask the children to choose two to compare and, using oil pastels, draw postcard-sized pictures of the homes.

- Use a digital camera to take photographs of the display with Christmas decorations added to the scene. Use the image to produce Christmas cards that the children could send to their family and friends.

Romeo and Juliet

This play was originally written by William Shakespeare and is one of the most famous love stories in the world. It is set in Verona with its narrow streets and high walls. The story is about Romeo and Juliet, two young people who fall deeply in love with each other at first sight. Romeo is a Montague and Juliet is a Capulet and their families are serious enemies. Although the play is a tragedy, there are many very amusing scenes with plenty of action and fighting. The ending is both tragic and powerful and has a very dramatic impact on the reader.

Starting Points

- Read *Romeo and Juliet (Shakespeare: The Animated Tales)* abridged by Leon Garfield and illustrated by Igor Makarov (published by Heinemann Young Books). Discuss the role of stage directions to convey location, setting and action concisely.

- Talk about the layout of a playscript in terms of cast of characters, use of brackets to convey expression and the names of the characters on the left-hand side of the page.

- Watch an animated film version of the play *Shakespeare – The Animated Tales of – Romeo And Juliet* (1992), or, even better, take the children to see a live performance.

Display

- A group of children should work together to create the background for the display board. Use grey poster paper and chalk pastels to create an evening scene.

- Cut out a balcony from grey paper. Add lines and colour to give it a stone-like appearance. Make it 3-D by curving it while it is being stapled to the display.

- Draw Romeo and Juliet. Use bright colours for Juliet and add her to the display on the balcony. Place Romeo below her looking up. Make him 3-D by raising him away from the display board.

- Cut out some leaves and plants from paper and make a garden along the bottom of the display.

- Add a suitable quote from the play and some curtains to either side of the display.

Further Activities

- Discuss Shakespeare's use of unfamiliar words and make a glossary to replace these words with words we would use today.

- Write a comparison between the play in print and its film version.

- Working in small groups, ask the children to prepare and rehearse a short section of the play to perform before an audience.

- Working in groups, ask the children to re-write the scene where Romeo and Juliet first meet. Offer the children the opportunity to perform their version, making sure that everyone in the group has a role to play.

Art and Design

- Discuss what either Romeo or Juliet might have worn to the masked ball. Design and paint a simple costume on paper. Use the paper design as a pattern for making a 2-D textile sample of the costume. Use calico as a base for stitching, but use more exotic fabrics – silk, satin, brocade, velvet and so on – for the actual garment. Use bold appropriate colours and embellish with embroidery stitches. Cut out the shapes and sew them onto the calico base.

Romeo and Juliet
The Party

Romeo enters the bustling party at the Capulet mansion. Candles are ablaze, lighting up the room. Masks, masks, everyone is wearing masks. Black slit eyes peep like voluptuous arrows of desire...Romeo has his eyes on fair Rosalyn but there is someone else as well – Romeo's true love.

Capulet: Welcome. Gentlemen, ladies come in with haste. Thou shalt have the best of times.

Mercutio: Dear friend, dance thou with the ladies!

Romeo: My dear friend, I wait for fair Rosalyne.

Juliet walks past Romeo in search of Paris.

Romeo: Who might this beautiful lady be?

Juliet: If thou must know I am Juliet.

Romeo: *(Over the sound of the music)* That is a lovely name ...Juliet.

- Share the children's ideas about their costumes and make comments about their choices of fabric, colour and embellishment. Discuss where they might wear similar costumes today.

- Design an invitation to the ball. Discuss what could be used as a family symbol and include it in the decoration of the invitation. Use A4 card and decorate around the edges to frame the invite.

A Midsummer Night's Dream

This play was originally written by William Shakespeare and tells a tale full of magic, intrigue and confusion. The story is about two young men, Demetrius and Lysander, and their two loves Helena and Hermia. Most of the play takes place in a woodland setting where Oberon and Titania are King and Queen of the Fairies. When some of the characters are given a magical potion taken from a flower, their emotions change and love is turned to hate and hate to love. The character of Bottom, whose head is transformed into the head of an ass, adds further confusion and delight to this magical play.

Starting Points

- Read *A Midsummer Night's Dream (Shakespeare: The Animated Tales)* abridged by Leon Garfield and illustrated by Elena Prorokova. In the opening scene, we are told that Hermia's father is angry with her. Discuss this scene in depth with the children, asking them: *Why is Hermia's father, Egeus, angry with his daughter? Who does Hermia want to marry?*

- Watch the animated film version of the play *Shakespeare – The Animated Tales of – A Midsummer Night's Dream* (1992) and compare it to the book.

- Discuss how the characters are presented through dialogue and action and how the setting is communicated to the reader.

Display

- Cover a display board in light green paper. Make a large tree trunk from paper to go down one side of the display and let the branches and roots frame the top and bottom of the display. Raise it away from the board to give a 3-D effect. Use thick paint to give texture to the trunk.

- Cut out some leaves from green card/fabric and add detail with paint. Add to the branches on the display.

- Make a nest by weaving either paper or fabric and then cutting it to shape. Add it to the display. Add some twigs and fill it with straw.

- Make Titania and Bottom. Use stitched tights for their faces and fabric for their clothes. Make their heads 3-D and add cut-out fabric clothes. Give Titania a crown and use felt or fur fabric for Bottom's ass head. Place them in the nest.

- Add some texture to the background by using a thick brush and thick paint for grass and flowers, make tissue paper or fabric flowers and add them to the display along with paper/fabric/collage leaves.

- Make some fairies from fabric with glossy wings and add them flying above Titania.

Further Activities

- Ask the children to create a story plan for the play including setting, characters, beginning, middle, ending, conflicts and resolutions. This will help them to sequence the story.

- Take a section of the play and, working in groups, practise playing the parts by following the stage directions and the emotions conveyed through the dialogue. Perform to the rest of the class.

- The children could write a short scene from the play using some of Shakespeare's unfamiliar words where appropriate.

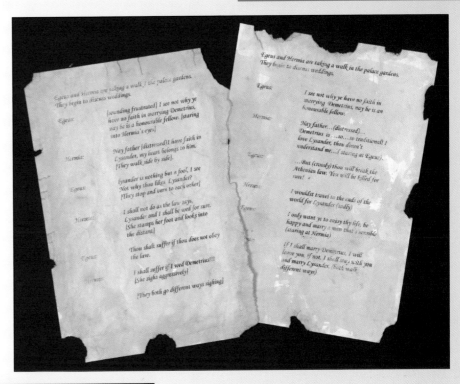

Art and Design

- In this play there are several references to birds and animals. Discuss these and select a few that might be suitable to interpret through masks, for example lion, ass, bear, raven, dove. In groups, make papier mâché or modroc masks of the creatures and use collage materials to decorate them.

- Much of the play is set in woodland. Work within the green colour family and, using pastels, draw an imaginary woodland scene. Frame it and decorate the frame using fabric and thread to make leaves and flowers.

- Provide some flowers and create a still life arrangement that the children could record in their sketchbooks. Use several different media to record the sketches – charcoal, sketch pencils, chalk and oil pastels, watercolour paints. Use a viewfinder to zoom in on an area of the sketch and make an enlarged abstract drawing of the selected area. Fill in the detail using contrasting colours. Mount the abstract section reproduced four times and rotated to create an interesting image.

Silver

Slowly, silently, now the moon
Walks the night in her silver shoon;
This way, and that, she peers, and sees
Silver fruit upon silver trees;
One by one the casements catch
Her beams beneath the silvery thatch;
Couched in his kennel, like a log,
With paws of silver sleeps the dog;
From their shadowy cote the white breast peep
Of doves in silver-feathered sleep;
A harvest mouse goes scampering by,
With silver claws, and silver eye;
And moveless fish in the water gleam,
By silver reeds in a silver stream.

Walter de la Mare

Silver

In the poem on page 54, the poet uses a range of figurative language to depict how the moon's silvery light is reflected on the surrounding countryside. The reader is presented with vivid images of the moon's silvery glow as it cascades over both nature and buildings alike. Personification is used to convey the moon as a beautiful woman in a silver gown and leaves the reader with a feeling of serenity and calm.

Starting Points

- Read *Silver* by Walter de la Mare (from *The Book of 1000 Poems: Classic Collection for Children* published by Collins).

- In this poem, we are given a glimpse of a more tranquil world, which is wrapped in the moon's silver light. Discuss the different images that are mentioned, such as the trees, the fruit, the doves, a harvest mouse and the stream full of fish.

- Walter de la Mare uses figurative language such as personification, alliteration, simile and repetition to create a vivid effect. Discuss these devices, which are used to create such a dramatic and memorable scene.

- Pose the following questions after reading and discussing the poem: *What is the poem about? What are the animals mentioned in the poem? What does the word 'scampering' tell you about the movement of the mouse? Why is silver repeated throughout the poem?*

Display

- Sponge a blue background with grey/pale blue/silver paint and cover a display board.

- Add a black and silver border.

- Cut out a large white moon and add it to the top of the display.

- Use fabric to add a large tree trunk to the side of the display and paint it with brown paint.

- Make a river using thick foil card and add it to the display.

- Make some doves out of card with tissue paper wings and place near the tree.

- Make some collage fish. Paint and embellish and add to the display.

- Sew some fabric and collage mice. Cut out some strips of green paper and add to the display as grass. Hide the mice in the grass.

More Design Ideas

- Paint a stream with a reflected moon in it.

- Paint some ghostly trees, raising them away slightly for a 3-D effect. Place larger tree trunks towards the front and smaller, paler ones towards the back. Make these flat and not 3-D. Add moonlight to one side of the trees.

- Add some grass using thick flat brushes and thin light green paint for a ghostly effect.

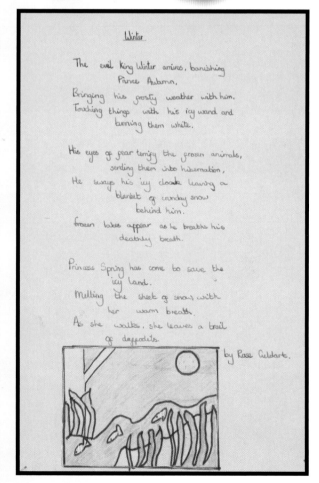

Further Activities

- Write individual poems on the same theme using personification, simile, repetition, alliteration and active verbs to create just the right mood. Ask the children to revise their poems and read them aloud individually.

- Ask the children to look up in a dictionary the old-fashioned words used by the poet such as 'casement', 'silver shoon', 'couched' and 'silvery thatch'. They could write a short descriptive piece about a cottage in the middle of a wood with a stream full of fish and a dog sleeping in its kennel on a moonlit night. They should try to capture its stillness and quaintness by using similar words to reflect a sense of past times.

- Place the children's poems around the display or in a special anthology in the school library for others to read.

Art and Design

- Look at pictures/paintings/photographs of doves – stationary and moving, perching, walking and flying. Discuss their shape, form and line. Concentrate on the patterns produced by their feathers. Using papier mâché or clay, make some doves. Add detail with paint/clay tools or collage materials. Display them in birdcages, either real or constructed from card, wood and/or wire.

- Look at paintings/pictures depicting moonlit nights, trees and forests. Sketch a simple collaborative picture of the woods in the moonlight and use collage materials to fill in the detail. Pay attention to the direction of the moonlight and add the 'shine' accordingly. Use silver acrylic paint, glitter/glitter glue, sequins, beads and anything else that sparkles to add atmosphere.

- Discuss the fish in the poem. On card, draw the outline of a moveless fish. Use lots of collage materials to add texture and detail to the fish. Make a mini table-top display of the fish on a pond in the moonlight.

Over De Moon

Dere's a man on de moon
He's skipping and stuff,
Dere's a man on de moon
He looks very tuff,
Dere's a man on de moon
An he's all alone,
Dere's a man on de moon
His wife is at home.

He's dancing around
To real moony music,
He carries his air
He knows how to use it,
He waves to his wife
Still on Planet E,
She's waving back
But he cannot see.

De man on de moon is so clever,
He has sum ideas to persue,
His chewing gum can last fe ever
His fast food is already chewed.

Dere's a man on de moon
He has a spaceship,
Dere's a man on de moon
An we payed fe it,
Dere's a man on de moon
His mission ain't done,
Dere's a man on de moon
He's after de Sun.

Benjamin Zephaniah

Over De Moon

The poem *Over De Moon* is about a man who has landed on the moon and is obviously enjoying himself. Benjamin Zephaniah tells us that this astronaut is very clever and that he has an important mission to complete. However, we are reminded that we have paid for his journey into space and that although he has reached his destination, the mission is not complete, as he now wants to explore the Sun.

Starting Points

- Read aloud the rap poem *Over De Moon* from *Talking Turkeys* by Benjamin Zephaniah (published by Puffin). Discuss the content of the poem and check that the children understand the meaning of each stanza.

- *Over De Moon* has a very definite beat and a clear rhyming pattern. Point out to the children that in the first and last stanzas, the first line is repeated every second line, like a chorus.

- This poem is great for performance and lends itself to movement and dance. Discuss with the children how they could make up simple dance routines to link in with the beat of the poem and its content. Put the children into groups to practise the rap and dance.

- Perform the poem and dance routines to the class. Alternatively, perform the whole poem together as a class in an assembly.

Display

- Cover a display board in black paper and splatter it with silver/white paint. Add a silver border.

- Create the moon – cut a large circle out of white fabric, like satin or other shiny material. Make some craters using three layers of fabric/paper/doilies/felt and add buttons/sequins/milk bottle tops. Stitch these through the middle onto the moon, adding further texture. Slightly stuff the moon as you add it to the display.

- Make some more planets in varying sizes using pastels – oil/chalk. Add simple embellishment and then stick to the board.

- Design an A3-sized spaceman using collage materials and place him going away from the moon towards the planets.

- Make three or four rockets using tubes of varying sizes. Decorate with brightly coloured paper/fabric. Add flames of tissue paper/fabric strips and add to the display board.

- Add a title, using white or silver letters, around the moon.

More Display Ideas

- Cover a display board in black paper. Paint some stars using silver/white paint in various sizes. Cut out and stick them onto the black background. Make the surface of the moon look textured by sponging areas in two shades of grey.

- Suspend the rockets in front of the display.

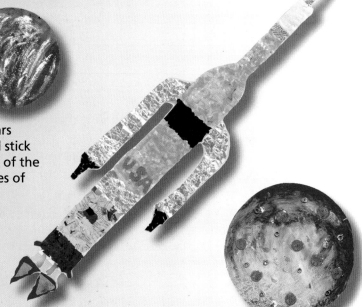

Further Activities

- The poem has a strong Jamaican influence and the language is simple but effective. Some of the spelling of words are deliberately incorrect and convey more of a Jamaican sound. Encourage the children to write some Jamaican-style poetry.

- Using Benjamin Zephaniah's poem *Over De Moon* as a model, ask the children to write two stanzas that have the same rhyming pattern as his first and fourth stanzas. Perform these poems to an audience, in groups of four, rather like a band, and use dance routines created by the children to add a dramatic flair.

- Using a digital camera, take photographs of the performances and display along with the poems.

Art and Design

- Discuss weightlessness and the way in which astronauts move in space. Do a large line drawing of an astronaut, concentrating on using flowing and overlapping lines and shapes. Ask the children to annotate their drawings and explain their use of shape.

- Discuss the difference in speed of a rocket and an astronaut and the ways in which line, shape and colour can be used to express the idea of movement. On A3 sketch paper, draw the outline of a rocket and use collage material to fill in the detail.

- Draw a series of planets on A3 card. Cut circles out of coloured paper, foil and doilies and stick them onto the planets. Add bottle tops, old coins and washers to give texture to the planets. Cut them out and arrange them in a 'galaxy' on a display board.

- Look at photographs and pictures of astronauts and identify the ways in which figures and forms in space move. On brightly coloured paper, ask the children to do a simple drawing of a moving figure. Cut the figures out and arrange them in an overlapping sequence to produce a collaborative, abstract picture.

The Pied Piper of Hamelin

Once more he stepped into the street;
And to his lips again
Laid his long pipe of smooth straight cane;
And ere he blew three notes (such sweet
Soft notes as yet musician's cunning
Never gave the enraptured air)
There was a rustling, that seemed like a bustling
Of merry crowds justling at pitching and hustling,
Small feet were pattering, wooden shoes clattering,
Little hands clapping and little tongues chattering,
And, like fowls in a farm-yard when barley is scattering,
Out came the children running.
All the little boys and girls,
With rosy cheeks and flaxen curls,
And sparkling eyes and teeth like pearls,
Tripping and skipping, ran merrily after
The wonderful music with shouting
    and laughter.

An extract from
The Pied Piper of Hamelin
by Robert Browning

The Pied Piper of Hamelin

In Robert Browning's narrative poem *The Pied Piper of Hamelin*, the story is told through a combination of dialogue and narrative verse. It begins with the people of Hamelin, who are in a very distressed state, arriving at their Town Hall to complain about the rats that are causing havoc everywhere. An important council meeting is held to discuss the problem of the rats and during this a most unusual looking man, a Pied Piper, appears and claims to be able to get rid of them by using his magical powers. The Mayor offers him a thousand guilders to do this. The Pied Piper plays a haunting tune and the rats follow him, as if in a trance, to the water's edge and plunge in. All the rats drown, except for one who lives to tell the tale. However, when the Mayor refuses to pay the Pied Piper an even greater calamity happens.

Starting Points

- Read the poem, *The Pied Piper of Hamelin* by Robert Browning (published by Orchard Books), and focus the children on Browning's use of figurative language to create a vivid image of the scene.

- In the poem, Browning tells the reader that the Pied Piper usually plays his pipe to help to get rid of harmful creatures. We find out later, that he is also prepared to use his musical talent as a form of retribution against the townspeople when they refuse to pay him the thousand guilders. Ask the children for their views on the Pied Piper. Do they think what he did was right?

- The ending of the poem is very mysterious and suggests that the children, who were led out of Hamelin by the Pied Piper, never returned. Discuss the language that gives the impression of this mystery and the ending of the poem in which the children eventually emerge in some far-off land, dressed in an outlandish way and with very different customs.

Display

- Back a display board with blue paper on the top half, and brown paper on the bottom half.
- Draw some buildings and paint them. Cut them out and place them in the top half of the display.

- Using a digital camera, take photographs of groups of the children. Discuss these with the children and ask them to think about their own images and then to draw themselves.

- Use pieces of old tights and stuffing to mould their heads. Stitch on buttons or beads for eyes and add other facial details with stitches or marker pens. Add coloured wool for hair. Make a slightly larger Pied Piper using the same method.

- Choose brightly coloured fabrics and stick cut-out clothes onto the drawn figures.

- Place the completed figures onto the background and create a busy group of happy dancing children. Add the Pied Piper to one side of the display.

- Cut out some pebble shapes in a variety of brown fabrics and add them to the empty spaces on the road area of the display.

- Create a border using musical notes cut from black paper and coins cut from foil and add to the top half of the display.

- Make some large rats by cutting two shapes out of felt and stitching them together with big, bold stitches. Add some stuffing before the final stitches are added. Add beads for eyes, thread for whiskers and string for tails. Place these rats on the border of the bottom half of the display.

More Display Ideas

- Create an alternative background for the display by using thick brushes to paint an area large enough to cover the top third of the display board. Use bold brush strokes to give the impression of the buildings.

- Add a border to the display by making some large coins using brown wax crayons and a light yellow paint wash and musical notes cut out of black paper.

Further Activities

- In the poem, Browning gives a colourful description of what the Pied Piper looked like. Ask the children to write a descriptive piece about the Pied Piper's appearance and illustrate it.

- Write another verse that would fit the poem to create another exciting episode about the children's adventures in their new land. Use the following as the first line: *When, lo, as they reached the mountain-side.* Follow the same rhyming pattern as in the poem, using three rhyming couplets followed by four lines, where the first line rhymes with the third and the second line with the fourth.

- Write an alternative ending to the poem, in which the children manage to escape from the mountain-side and tell their parents about how the Piper's music enchanted them.

Art and Design

- Talk about the countryside around Hamelin and create a collage using a variety of textiles.

- Choose some music that represents the various moods in the story, such as fear of the rats, joy at the arrival of the Pied Piper and excitement as the rats follow him. Give the children a large piece of plain paper and some wax crayons and let them draw what they feel when they listen to the music. Encourage bold, simple strokes with the crayons.

- Ask the children to draw their own faces on a piece of calico and then stitch in the detail using a variety of threads.

- Discuss the historical period of the time of the poem and make some 3-D houses. Discuss the common features of Tudor houses, like the slightly larger first floor. Working in groups subdivided into pairs, draw the design of the house on paper. Then build a simple frame using wood cut to length and stuck together with a glue gun. Cut the walls and roof from thick white card and add to the framework of the house. Paint the beams on the outside of the houses and add further detail using paint, coloured pencils and felt for flowers, windows, doors and so on. Paint the roof yellow/brown.

Lullaby

Someone would like to have you for her child
but you are mine.
Someone would like to rear you on a costly mat
but you are mine.
Someone would like to place you on a camel blanket
but you are mine.
I have you to rear on a torn mat.
Someone would like to have you as her child
but you are mine.

Akan, Africa

© Belair

Lullaby

The poem *Lullaby* evokes images of wealth and poverty. Sometimes the things we love the most become worn and frayed because they are used and not just admired. The poem comes from another culture, one in which life is simpler and material wealth is not valued as highly as it is in ours. It simply says that, in spite of her lack of material riches, the love of a mother for her young child is the greatest gift of all.

Starting Points

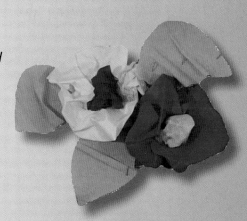

- Read the poem *Lullaby*, Akan, Africa from *Classic Poems to Read Aloud* selected by James Berry (published by Kingfisher).

- Discuss the poem's message about the importance of love, in this case a mother's love for her young child. Ask the children some thought-provoking questions: *What are the real riches in life? Do you need to give material things to show you love someone? When you really care about another person, do you think they become your treasure? Why is the title of this poem so effective?*

- Encourage the children to think of something or someone who is very precious, perhaps a brother or a sister or a special toy. Discuss these and focus on why they are so important.

- Talk about the structure of the poem and how the poet uses repetition of an alternative line rhyme in *'But you are mine.'* to convey such a strong emotion. Can the children find examples of this in other poetry?

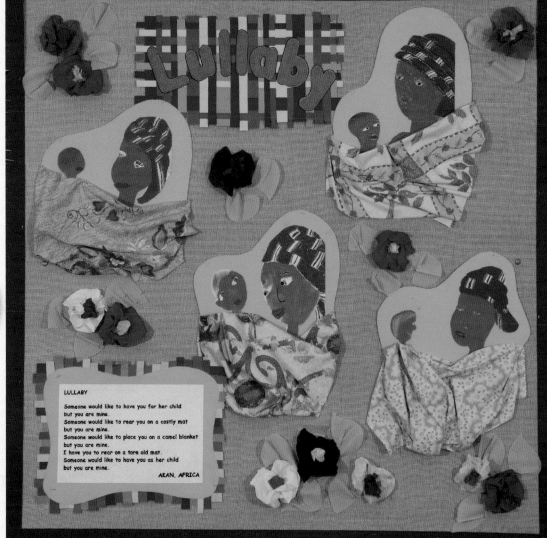

LULLABY

Someone would like to have you for her child
but you are mine.
Someone would like to rear you on a costly mat
but you are mine.
Someone would like to place you on a camel blanket
but you are mine.
I have you to rear on a torn old mat.
Someone would like to have you as her child
but you are mine.

AKAN, AFRICA

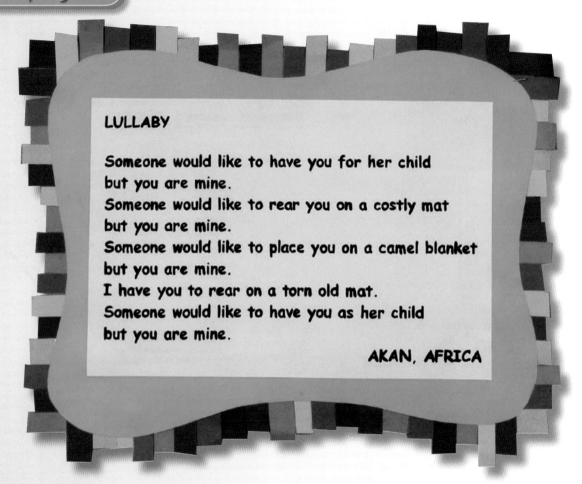

LULLABY

Someone would like to have you for her child
but you are mine.
Someone would like to rear you on a costly mat
but you are mine.
Someone would like to place you on a camel blanket
but you are mine.
I have you to rear on a torn old mat.
Someone would like to have you as her child
but you are mine.

AKAN, AFRICA

- Look at double portraits of a mother and child in paintings, photographs and book illustrations, and in other contexts.

- Ask the children to sketch a double portrait of a mother and child, which shows a close relationship between them.

- Add colour with chalk pastels and cut out around the outline.

- Cover a display board with hessian.

- Arrange the portraits on the display board.

- Wrap a vibrant piece of cloth around the double portraits to show their closeness.

- Place the poem on the display.

- Add a bright, fringed paper border.

- Create a title made using hessian letters stuck to a woven paper background.

- Discuss the display with the children.

More Design Ideas

- Create an alternative background by weaving together strips of paper.

- Place a simple, frayed hessian border around the display.

- Use a number of different double portrait images – perhaps some of the children and a family member or friend.

- Add some of the children's poems to the display.

Further Activities

- Re-read the poem *Lullaby* with the class and focus on how it reflects the customs of another culture. In traditional African tribes, mothers carry their babies with them wherever they go. Also, women tend to wrap their clothes around their babies, often covering over their heads with brightly coloured cloths. Discuss these differences.

- In the poem, the mother talks about her deep love for her child. Using the poem as a starting point, ask the children to write a letter from the mother to her young child, which expresses her feelings.

- Using the poem as a model for poetry writing, produce individual lullabies, which depict children's treasures.

- Produce an anthology of poetry and keep it in the library for others to share.

- Organise a poetry reading session for other children to hear the poems performed.

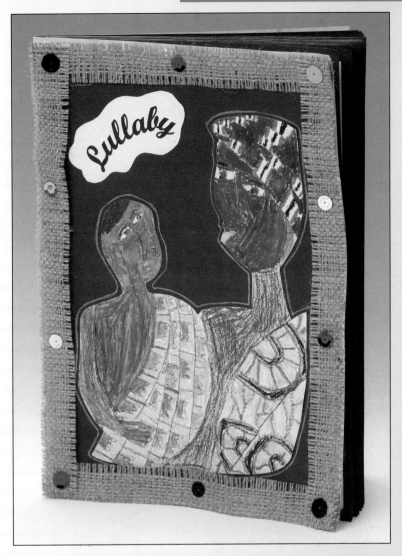

Art and Design

- Look at images of double portraits in book illustrations and in paintings and discuss the composition in terms of the possible relationship between the two people.

- Ask the children to choose one of the double portraits from a book illustration and do a quick sketch outline in chalk. Develop the composition in mixed media, combining paint mixed with sand and coloured inks. Discuss and compare the children's work.

- Using a digital camera, take a photograph of two children posing. Using the photograph as a starting point, draw a very simple outline of the two children on an A3 sheet of coloured paper. Using fabric that has texture rather than colour, for example velvet, silk, calico, hessian, corduroy, in natural creams or beige, build up a collage of the two children. Add some wool or torn fabric and add other features with stitches.

My Pet Grass Snake

Casssssssandra is my pet grass snake
She likes to lounge by the pond
Eyeing up amphibians
Of which she is rather fond.

She eases her length into the water
With the stealth of a midnight thief
It matters not that her prey
Is concealed beneath a leaf.

She attacks with the speed of a
flashgun
And swallows it breast to dorsal
And even before it's halfway down
She's after the next froggy morsel.

Maurice Waller

My Pet Grass Snake

Maurice Waller's poem *My Pet Grass Snake* (see page 70) looks at the snake in an amusing way. It describes the movements of Cassandra, the pet grass snake, as she eagerly stalks her prey. The poem captures the character of the snake, which at first appears very relaxed, almost lazy, in her approach to catching her next meal. However, at the end of the poem, Cassandra attacks her target with a sudden gusto.

Starting Points

- Read the poem *My Pet Grass Snake* by Maurice Waller and discuss how in each verse the second and the fourth line rhyme.

- Pose how the use of onomatopoeia in the snake's name, Cassandra, creates an effective image. Ask the children for other examples of onomatopoeia and list these on the board.

- Pose the following questions: *Which words suggest that the snake is rather lazy? What does 'stealth' mean? Why is it a good word to use in connection with the word 'thief'? (The clue is hidden inside the word 'stealth'.) Do snakes chew their food? What information does it give in the poem to explain this?*

- The poem describes two very different ways in which the snake moves. Discuss how and why she moves in these two ways.

Display

- Cover a display board with green paper and add a yellow, curved, cut border.

- Cut a pond shape out of card/foil. Cover it with blue organza/netting cut larger than the pond shape. Tuck the fabric underneath the pond shape and secure. Fold and scrunch the fabric on the surface of the pond to give it texture.

- Make some water lily pads using thick card, cut to shape and sponged with green paint. Stick these onto bits of wood and then onto the pond so that they are slightly raised. Add some tissue paper flowers to the pond.

- Make a 3-D snake by stuffing a leg made of tights with tissue paper. Add green triangles of cut paper to the tights as skin. Place the snake crawling towards the water.

- Create some 3-D frogs by cutting out a simple frog shape in two pieces of fabric, stitching them together and stuffing slightly. Decorate the fabric with paint and sponges/brushes. Hide the frogs beneath the water lilies.

- Add some grass to the background using thick paint and brush strokes.

- Shred some green tissue paper and add it to the wet paint. Make some more tissue paper flowers and add these to the background.

- Add a title made out of letters that look like snakes. Use two contrasting colours. Cut large letters out of one colour and add stripes/triangles of a contrasting colour on top.

71

Further Activities

- Using the same rhyming pattern as *My Pet Grass Snake*, ask the children to write their own poems about an unusual pet. Include an example of onomatopoeia in the poems.

- Ask the children to read aloud or to recite their poems by heart with a focus on the use of onomatopoeia and rhyming patterns to create effect.

- The children could write another verse for *My Pet Grass Snake*, using the same rhyming pattern and tone. Rehearse and read the whole poem, including the additional verse, with appropriate expression.

Art and Design

- Look at pictures of snakes and discuss the patterns that can be seen on their skins. Using paper, ask the children to make a simple repeat pattern using two contrasting colours.

- Make a papier mâché model of unusual pets and discuss ways of adding texture to the model.

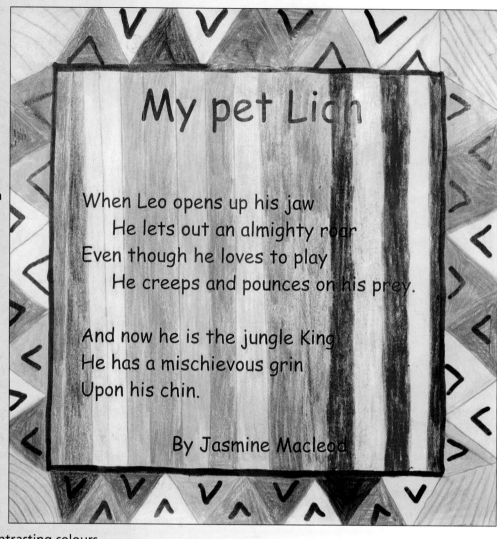

My pet Lion

When Leo opens up his jaw
    He lets out an almighty roar
Even though he loves to play
    He creeps and pounces on his prey.

And now he is the jungle King
He has a mischievous grin
Upon his chin.

By Jasmine Macleod

- The children could cut out some fabric water lily leaves, add glue to the middle and stick them onto A4 card. Hide pictures of frogs or other garden creatures cut out from magazines or drawn by the children in amongst the leaves.

- Discuss other creatures that may use the pond and illustrate these with watercolours.

72